Apple Watch Series 5

Learn Everything You Need To Know About Apple Watch

Philip Knoll

Printed in the United States of America

Graw-Hill Publishing House

2 Penn Plaza,

NY 10121

New York

USA

ISBN: 9781693614361

Dedication

To Philip parents, patty jean, James Knoll a nd my loving wife and son Diana, Kevin wh o are a constant source of love, encouragement ,and positive energy.

Table of Contents

INTENSIONALLY LEFT BLANK

CHAPTER 1

Introduction

I want to thank you and congratulate you on downloading this book " Apple Watch Series 5 : Learn Everything You Need to Know about Apple Watch".

This book an update version that contains proven steps and strategies, tips, and tricks on how to learn everything you need to know about Apple Watch.

When the Apple Watch was initially released in 2015, it wasn't exactly clear what problems it solved or who would be its demographic group. Johnny, the company directors, admitted that during an interview with him.

Apple's Watch has changed a lot in its short life

A brief history of the Apple Watch

*T*im Cook initially announced the Apple Watch in September 2014, and the first of Apple's Watch wearable shipped the subsequent year on April. Since its birth, the Apple Watch has deeply changed—specifically from the way it sold initially. During that time, Apple has sold 33 million Apple Watch devices ever since 2015, making it the #1 best-selling watch of wearable tech in the world.

Four years is a time in the tech universe, although, and a lot can happen. However, since 2015, Apple has updated Apple every year, refining the design and introducing new features and scientific innovations. Health and fitness are at the core of what Apple Watch is all about. But as you'll see in this section, the improvements Apple has made in its most recent are genuinely incredible. Let's take a look at the Apple Watch to see how far it's come.

The Original Apple Watch (2015)

The first Apple Watch didn't come with a Series number, as successive Apple Watches would. However, there were three different lines of Apple smart Watch when it is out. The first was modestly called "Apple Watch"–this was the everyman edition that was made up of stainless steel. At that moment, there was the Apple Watch Sport *with bands and an aluminum build made to appeal to athletes. And lastly, there was the Apple Watch Edition made from 18-karat gold.*

As you may probably predict from the gold used to make the Apple Watch Edition, it sold as a fashion accessory and the price topped around $17,000. But unfortunately, the Apple Watch Edition didn't sell well at all and was dropped the subsequent year. The original Apple Watches came in 38mm and 42mm sizes and featured Wi-Fi and Bluetooth only. Internet access is required when pairing with an iPhone. All models also had a Digital Crown, Digital Touch, Multi-Touch, Force Touch, and Side button. All also sported an optical heart sensor.

The following year 2016, Apple unveiled its first update to the Apple Watch team list. As already stated, gone was the expensive Apple Watch Edition made from 18-Karat gold. They also got rid of the moniker "Apple Watch Sport."

Apple watch series I &2

As an alternative, Apple renamed an updated version of the Sport because it had an aluminum build, the Apple Watch Series 1. They reduced the price to make it the entry-level model that is affordable for most Apple products fans. It retained the same features that the original Apple Watch had: a Digital Crown, Digital Touch, Multi-Touch, Force Touch, and Side button.

Apple introduced the new Apple Watch Series 2 that year. This model again has an aluminum body as well, but, its main distinguishing point was that, unlike the Series 1, the Series 2 had built-in GPS. It meant no needed for the iPhone to pair with your Apple Watch device to get location data.

Apple Watch Series 3 (2017)

In 2017, Apple introduced the Apple Watch and renamed it Apple Watch Series 3. The *difference here is that the Series 3 added a cellular option. For the first time in Apple watch history,*

Apple watches series 3

the Watch itself could connect to its mobile Internet—further removing the need to pair the device with your iPhone.

Apple Watch Series 4 (2018)

The Apple Watch Series 4 unveiled in 2018; the Series 4 featured some most essential upgrades over the Series 3 lineup. The first difference is that Series 4 featured bigger screen displays. Instead

Apple watch series 4

of coming in 38mm and 42mm regular sizes, the Series 4 began in 40mm and 44mm sizes while retaining roughly the same footmark of the Series 3.

The other enormous improvement to Series 4 was the addition of an electrical heart sensor (ECG/EKG). This ECG lets users to check their heart rate at any time and if the Apple Watch detects a low or high cardiac rhythms heart rate, it alerts you—even when you don't feel any symptoms

Apple watch series 5

Honestly speaking, we'd have been surprised if the modern Apple wearable wasn't announced alone in the event, given that new versions have come out alongside new iPhones for years. The Apple Watch presently holds the title of the best-selling smartwatch in the world. And the Apple Watch 5 was the company's most elegant device produced in the recent time.

Apple knew it desired to create a super watch that would figure out what it would do after the fact. Following the launch, there was a list of issues that hampered the Apple Watch's abilities, relegating it to being a slow sidekick to the iPhone. It could not process much locally, offloading the majority of the work to the iPhone. Watch faces were quite limited, as were the complications that could run on them. Make the situation worse. It was slow to launch apps, and Siri was less than helpful. Developers, initially excited about Watch's prospects, began to flee the platform, with much pulling support in recent app updates. Over past years, Apple Watch hasn't seen more than incremental spec bumps. Apple is adding features like water resistance, faster processors, and cellular as on where Apple Watch excelled. On the outside, the Apple watch design remained largely the same for three years. It's one of the most frequent questions among people looking to get the Apple Watch for the first time what does this swatch do?

When it comes to smartwatches, Apple's got it right. Other wearables exist, but most are beautiful hit-or-miss when it comes to the right balance of functionality and performance. And none, no matter your perspective, fit in the iPhone the way the Apple Watch does. It's got an unfair advantage, given both gadgets come from under the same corporate roof. But that interaction also explains why the Apple Watch is such a great wearable, and why the $ 400-and-up Series 5 is a welcome *improvement compared to the Series 4. It increases some cool gimmicks you'll either love or hate, and some much-needed health tracking options.*

So what's changed, precisely? Well, not much, at least in terms of looks. The Series 5 uses the same physical design as the Series 4. Inside, a new S5 processor and 32GB of internal storage — double of the Series 4's 16GB — makes the watch feel more impressively responsive. There are some modern finishes like titanium and the pricey white ceramic if you're feeling decorative. The new Apple Watch Series 5 fits all the watch bands of the same size that came before it. Meaning that you won't have to deal with any unexpected incompatibility issues (the older 38 and 42mm bands will still work on your larger 40mm and 44mm Apple Watch).

One significant difference you will notice is the Apple Watch's new always-on feature, which keeps the display active even when you're not looking at it. Finally, the Apple Watch Series 5 tells time, all the time, and regularly.

Have you wondered why many want to get the latest series 5 of Apple watch? Do you want to learn the best ways, tips, and tricks so that you may utilize your watch and maximize its efficiency? You are on the right course in determining the most effective ways to utilize your Apple Watch using this book. Thanks, once again, for downloading this book, I hope you enjoy it.

10 September 2019 Apple event

As we expected, the Apple Watch Series 5 was launch on September 10 alongside the new iPhone 11, and we were not disappointed. Apple's new smartwatch has been shown to the world on 10 September 2019.

We'd have been surprised if the modern Apple wearable wasn't announced alone in the event, given that new versions have come out alongside new iPhones for years. The Apple Watch presently holds the title of the best-selling smartwatch in the world. And the Apple Watch 5 was the company's most elegant device produced in the recent time.

This book contains all that you need to know about the latest models. We've collected a list of all the features coming in the new Apple Watch Series 5 - and we've gotten first hands information with the device.

Watch OS 6 release date, and features

The Apple Watch Series 5 announced during the company's September 10 event, along with the next iPhone in California. Hermes edition on sale September 20, while Nike version on sale October 4.

It's publically coming out on September 20, starting at $398 for the GPS-only model in 40mm and $428 for the 44mm version. The cellular model in 40mm starts at $498 and can go up to $528 for the 44mm model.

The Apple Watch Series 5's starting prices are for the 100% recycled aluminum case, which comes in several finishes: Gold, Space Black, and a Polished gray hue.

You can pick it up in stainless steel for a more excellent price - $698 with a sport loop or sport band, $748 with a Milanese loop, or $798 with a leather loop. Titanium, in light and dark finishes, starts at $798 with a sport loop and goes up to $898 with a leather loop.

The watch will come in a Ceramic white finish, starting at $1,298 with a sport loop and going up to $1,398 with a leather loop.

There are modern Nike models with additional bands, loops, and faces. There are Hermes models, with Space Black stainless steel cases and noir leather bands. Apple didn't clearly announce whether these models would be available in both GPS-only and cellular.

The Apple Watch Series 5 has come on with an Always-On Retina display. Which, well, never turns off - it just dims when you're not using it, so time and complications (notifications) are always visible. Just rotate your watch to face you to light it back up.

It has the capability with a new display driver, power efficiency, and ambient light sensor. That works with software to deliver always-on display while not lessening the watch's 18-hour battery life.

All the watch faces have carefully tuned to the display. The workout app has been tweaked to show stats and exercise data endlessly.

Compass and updated Maps app

The Apple Watch Series 5 has enhanced its built-in compass, which now displays latitude, longitude, elevation, and inclination angles. The Maps app has also been reorganized to show you which way you're facing.

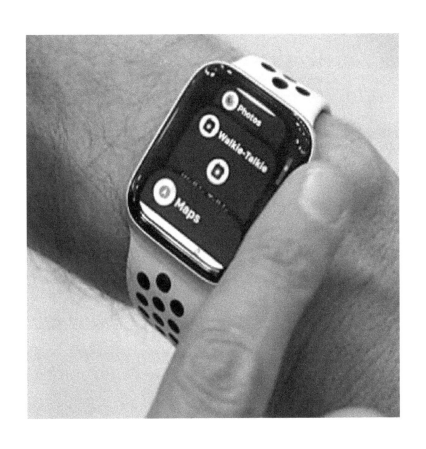

Safety features and health tracking of series 5

The Apple Watch Series 5 has improved the safety features in the watch with fall detection, Medical ID, and emergency SOS. Emergency SOS has also developed: the cellular version can directly call emergency services in many international countries by holding the Watch crown button-down in an emergency.

During this year's event, Apple announced the health studies it's helping with by associating with research institutes and hospitals for heart, hearing, and women's health, including menstrual cycle monitoring.

Users can participate in the upcoming Apple Research app, which is coming to Apple Watches later. To protect individual confidentiality, the data submitted can't access by Apple staff.

Despite the fact we didn't hear much about watch OS6, we're enthusiastically anticipating its release, which could come together with the Apple Watch 5's release on 20 September 2019.

The great feature in the latest version is the introduction of an App Store straight on the Apple watch - credibly, so you can use it without even needing a phone as a go-between.

WatchOS 6 carry on the phone-detaching trend with three new unrelated watch apps that are wrist bound versions of existing iPhone apps:

- *Apple Books*
- *Voice Memos*
- *Calculator.*

Using a display that is now always on, Apple Watch 5 is there for you never like before. Faces and complications allow you to see the information that matters most to you without raising your wrist. Cases are accessible in a range of materials engineered by Apple, including 100 percent recycled aluminum and, for the first time, titanium. Match with several bands you like and create a blend that is entirely personalized for you.

Always-On Retina display.

It is no longer necessary to raise your wrist or touch the screen to see the time. Or other information on your Apple watch face, because the new display never sleeps. If you are on the bike or counting the minutes in a meeting, all you need to do is glance to find the time or your workout metrics right on your watch screen.

A screen as amazing as the day is long. Continue all day with all-day battery life, hardware and software have to work in synchronization.

The screen display dims when your wrist is down; however, the key features, like watch hands, stay visible at all times. Touching the face or raising your wrist brings the whole thing back to full brilliance.

Customize your watch face

You can personalize Apple watch face by selecting apps or shortcuts to features.

What we call complications (that allow you to see more at a glance and do more with a touch). There are hundreds to tap into, and some faces, such as Infographics, can house up to nine.

Infographic watch face with Timer, Weather, UV Index, Audiobooks, Noise Monitor, Compass, Activity, Cycle Tracking

Modular Compact watch face with: Date, Activity, Compass, analog clock dial

Meridian watch face with: World Clock, Earth, Moon, Solar

Infographic Modular watch face with: Favorite Contacts, Weather Conditions, Heart Rate, Breathe, Workout

Meridian watch face with: Weather Temperature, UV Index, Rain, Wind

Twenty-eight Apple Watch tips and tricks you should know

Whether you've just purchased your first or fifth Apple Watch, these tips and tricks would benefit you. There are a lot of things you can do with Apple Watch, beyond checking the time or sending messages alone.

Here are 28 miraculous tips and tricks about that new wearable device on your wrist!

General tips

1. Wake to your last-used app

When you flick your wrist, by default Apple Watch will wake and show the time automatically.

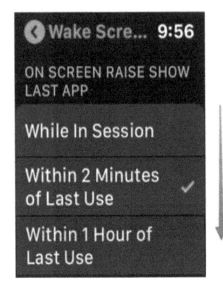 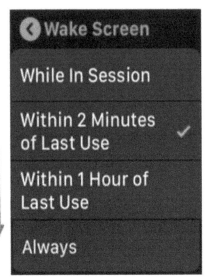

If you'd prefer to go back to whatever you were doing before it going to sleep, you can adjust that setting by going to Settings > General > Wake Screen.

Then, scroll down to the section On Screen Raise Show Last. Sets include While in Sessions, within two Minutes of Last Use, Within 1 Hour of Last Use, and Always.

2. Make the on-screen text bigger

With your tiny device, sometimes, you want the option for larger text at your disposal. Apple watch makes this simple in its accessibility settings; to change the text on your Apple Watch.

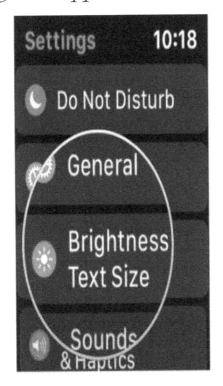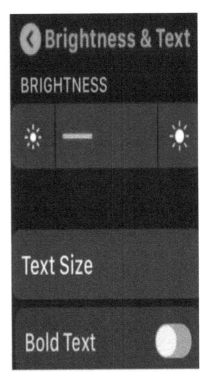

Apple Watch brightness and text size

Go to Settings > select Brightness and Text Size and adjust to your liking.

You can also select a specialty Big Text watch face if all you're interested in is seeing the time in large numerals format.

3. Mute or silent alerts with your palm

If you have enabled sound on the Apple Watch, you can keep it quiet from frustrating others with notification sounds. If it goes off in a place, you can cover the display with your hand for four seconds or more to instantly mute any sounds. To turn this on, you'll visit the Apple Watch app on your iPhone, and then go to My Watch > Sounds and Haptics > Cover to Mute.

4. Hide watch apps

To hide any third-party apps from displaying on your Apple Watch, go into the Apple

Watch app on your iPhone and ensure you're in the My Watch section. Scroll down to the unit called Installed on Apple Watch. Tap the apps you'd like to remove by toggling to the off position. Even though you've deleted their Watch interfaces, those apps will usually remain installed on your iPhone unless you delete them from that device.

Remove third-party apps

5. Find your iPhone with your Watch

If you can't find your iPhone? Don't bother about it — the Apple Watch can support you track it down. From your Apple Watch face, swipe up to activate Control Center. From there, tap the Ping iPhone button in blue to have it make a loud noise.

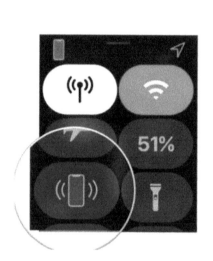 

Find iPhone on Apple Watch

6. Quickly access Zoom and VoiceOver

If you want to Zoom or VoiceOver to be readily available on your Apple Watch? You can also turn on the triple-click Accessibility shortcut to automatically activate either Zoom or VoiceOver. To do so, visit the Apple Watch app on the iPhone, then go to My Watch > General > Accessibility > Accessibility Shortcut. Then you can select which you'd like to activate on triple-click automatically.

Apple Watch voice over

Siri can turn VoiceOver on or off with a verbal command — ask your Watch.

7. Take a screenshot

If you want to remember that Digital Touch Activity achievement. You can take a screenshot on your Watch by speedily and simultaneously pressing both the side button and Digital Crown.

8. Force Apple Watch to restart

If your Watch is naughty, you can turn it off by pressing and holding the side button until you see the Power Off slider, then drag it across the screen. If your Apple Watch is entirely frozen, you can perform a force reboot autimatcally. By holding both the side button and Digital Crown for twelve seconds, until you see the Apple logo appear.

9. Save custom watch faces

Apple has come with the accessibility of not only can you customize. Watch's default faces by using Force Touch on the Apple Watch display, but you can also save customized faces for future usage. To do so, Force Touch on the Apple Watch display once, then swipe to the left and tap the button. You can customize the different models of your Apple watch face to liking.

To delete a custom watch face, swipe up.

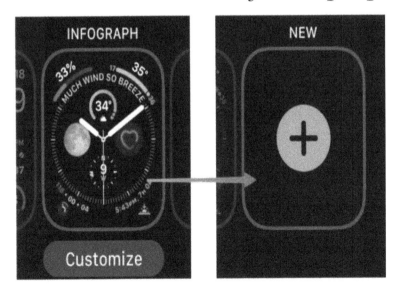

Create an apple watch face

10. Set your Watch five minutes faster

If you want like to be early for your appointments, you can manually set the watch face to show five minutes more quickly. That won't affect your alarms, notifications, or clocks from other countries, but it'll display on the Apple Watch face. To do this, go to Settings > Time > +0 min, and then turn the Digital crown to advance the time ahead up to 59 minutes.

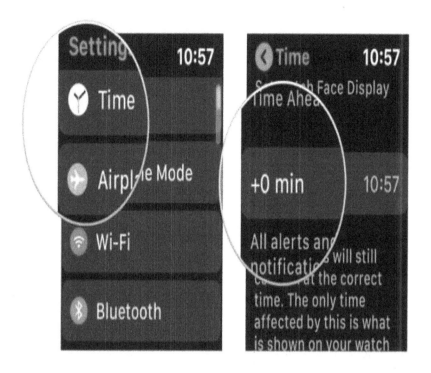

Apple Watch time advance

11. Turn off snooze for your watch alarms

Don't trust yourself about to wake up on time? You can also disable the Snooze button on the Apple device by going into the Alarm app on the device and tapping on the alarm time you'd like to modify. Toggle so snooze isn't an option.

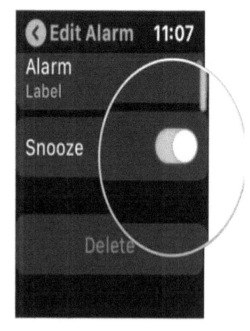

Apple Watch snooze

Communication

12. Pre-compose custom Messages responses

You should know that you can't type directly on your Apple Watch. Still, you can set up a few pre-composed responses through your iPhone that you can tap on during conversations to auto-send. To do this, visit the Apple Watch app, and then go to My Watch > Messages > Default Replies. You can also change this list and add/ remove pre-composed responses at any time you wish.

Default replies

13. Every time send your dictated text as audio

When you need to reply to a message with your voice, your Apple Watch support one of two choices: sending it as prescribed text or sending dictation as an audio clip. If you select that, your messages always send as audio clips or always as dictation. You can make this by visiting the Apple Watch app on your iPhone, and then going to My Watch > Messages > Audio Messages.

14. Share location to friend in Messages with Force Touch

Do you want to send a friend to your current location while you're out? From your Message conversation, Force Touch the display and tap Send Location.

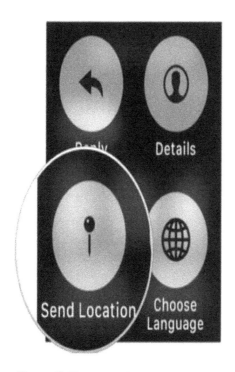 

Send Location

15. Hold a call until you can find your iPhone

While taking phone calls on, the Apple Watch is beautiful futuristic-feeling, it's not always practical. If you get a call on your Apple Watch that you want to pick up, but your phone's not within reach, and you don't want to start it on your Watch, you can tap

Answer on iPhone to place the call on hold until you can find your device. The one on the other end will hear a short repeated sound until you can get to your iPhone.

16. Turn on Walkie-Talkie

You want to activate the Walkie-Talkie feature on your new Apple Watch to use it. To do so, go into the Walkie-Talk application on the wearable device and turn on the Available toggle. Else, people won't be able to reach you using the tool.

Productivity

17. Clear your notifications with Force Touch

Although you can swipe left to delete a single notification from the Notifications screen, you can get rid of all your notification alerts in one tap. Firstly, swipe down from the display to access Notifications, and then Force Touch the show to bring up the Clear All option.

18. Flag Mail messages with Force Touch

There's no way to compose a new email on the Apple Watch outstanding to its relative impossibility as an email machine. Still, you can also flag messages you like to reply to later. Just Force Touch on a mail message, and then tap Flag.

19. Pick out what mailboxes show up on your Apple Watch

If you don't like to be overwhelmed with notifications and information from all your mailboxes? You can select specific mailboxes to display up on the Apple Watch from the iPhone application.

Just go to My Watch > Mail > Include Mail.

Included mail

20. Switch in-between Day and List views in Calendar

If you want to see what your day looks like — but also view items in a list? You can switch in-between Day and List views in the

Calendar by tapping a Force to Touch gesture on the screen while in the app.

21. Build your leaving time into Calendar alerts

If there's a location added to your calendar event, you can create a new alert to inform you when to leave that factors in driving or walking a distance along with traffic. To do so, make sure the specific event has the Travel Time switch enabled. You can do this on your iPhone by going to the Calendar app, tapping the event in inquiry, and going to Edit > Travel Time.

Apps

22. Use the Taptic Engine when you're getting new directions

Your Watch supports a range of beeps, buzzes, and movements to get your attention, but it doesn't stop with notifications. You can use the Taptic Engine to help navigate you around any city. When you're getting directions through the Watch, you'll receive a series of taps when you have to make a turn.

For a left turn, you'll get a series of two taps, played three times: tap-tap — tap-tap — tap-tap.

For a right turn, you'll get a steady beat of 12 taps: tap-tap-tap-tap-tap-tap-tap-tap-tap-tap-tap-tap

You'll also get a long vibration when you're on your last leg of the journey and when you arrive at your destination.

23. Stop directions with Force Touch

If you like your Watch to stop navigating? Use a Force Touch gesture at any point on the Maps app to cease directions.

24. Review your iPhone photos from Apple watch

The Camera app on your Watch allows you to use it as a remote display and shutter for photos. Still, you can also swiftly review any recent shots. That way, you should ensure you've gotten the perfect group shot before retrieving your iPhone.

25. Set a default city for your weather app

The Weather app on your Apple Watch can check a different of cities, such as your current Location. To change the default location setting, visit the Apple Watch app on your iPhone, and then go to My Watch > Weather > Default City.

26. Close your rings

Apple Watch raises your mood for the whole day long close your exercise rings. To find out how you're doing, bring up the Exercise app.

27. How to use Apple to watch ECG?

On the fourth-generation Watch, Cupertino has added the capability to check your ECG from your wearable watch. To do so, tap on the ECG applications on your Watch, and then hold your finger on the digital crown for at least 30 seconds while cardiac electrical signals are measured. Learn more about ECG in chapter 26.

28. Concentrate

In conclusion, you can also use the built-in breathe app to relax. In the app, use the Digital Crown to set how many minutes of

breaths you would like to keep track of.
Next, hit the Start and relax.

CHAPTER 2

Inside Apple watch series 5

*A*pple put as much care into engineering the case materials as we do the technology they contain. They now offer four decorative elements, including titanium. Each of the metals and the ceramic use were carefully engineered by

Apple to enhance their inherent qualities while bringing out a distinctive beauty.

- *Stainless Steel.*
- *Aluminum.*
- *Ceramic.*
- *Titanium.*

Stainless Steel.

Stainless steel is known for its durability and resistance to corrosion, and stainless steel is a principal of traditional watchmaking. This metal gave it a mirror-like finish and made it 80% harder using a specific cold-forging process of its invention.

Aluminum.

Apple Watch uses 7000 series aerospace-grade aluminum that is at once extremely strong and incredibly light. It is a similar alloy used in the iPhone XR. And now, the aluminum used in the Apple Watch Series 5 case is 100 % recycled.

Ceramic

Brilliant white through Apple engineered the ceramic to be scratch-resistant and extremely durable. Assuring it will maintain its stunning looks even after many years of wear.

Titanium.

The titanium is found in the most exclusive Apple watches, and titanium is reliable, lightweight, and beautiful. For the natural titanium finish, they developed a special surface coating that prevents yellowing, staining, and showing fingerprints. The Space Black is created with the same DLC process use for stainless steel, yielding an exquisite finish.

The Apple Watch bands.

Apple Watch bands are well designed to be easily interchangeable. They can slide on and off, so you can smoothly swap bands as you run from the gym to dinner.

Apple watch sizing guide

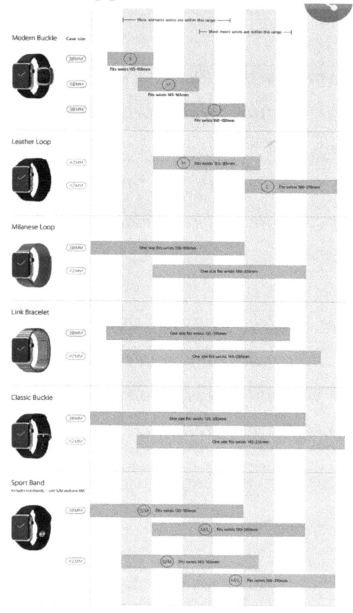

Apple watch sizing guide

Select from elegant leathers, high-performance fluoroelastomer, flexible nylon weaves, or metal bands if that's what you want. With many colors and clever clasps, your Apple Watch can be like a new watch, over and over again.

The technology that makes it tick.

Apple Watch Series 5 packs with capabilities into a footprint so small it's more like a fingerprint. Tucked the deceptively simple surface are many massive feats of engineering.

Ultra-low-power LTPO display. The low-temperature poly-silicon and oxide display structures. And reinvented pixel architecture that allows the screen refresh rate dip from 60Hz to a power-sipping 1Hz when the Apple watch is inactive. A new low-power driver, ultra-efficient power administration, and a new ambient light sensor work together so the display can stay at all times on with up to 18 hours of battery life. The S5 is a comprehensive System in Package (SiP), with the entire system fabricated onto a single component.

GPS Compass of Apple watch 5

Compass and location features.

The GPS built-in magnetometer detects the magnetic north then automatically adjusts to display true north, so you'll now identify which way you're facing in the Maps App. GPS works in combination with terrain data to tell you your current elevation, and this is great for outdoor workouts.

Apple Watch series 5, All-Day Battery Life, was tested by Apple in August 2019 using preproduction Apple Watch Series 5 (GPS). And Apple Watch Series 5 (GPS + Cellular), both paired with an iPhone; all devices tested with prerelease software. The battery life varies by use, cellular coverage, configuration, and other factors; actual results vary

Hands-on Health Monitor

Apple Watch encourages a healthier life. It can monitors your heart rate and let you know if something is wrong. It helps you keep track of women's menstrual cycle and taps if noise levels rise to the point that could impact your normal hearing. You can add complications like Breathe, Heart Rate, and Noise to your Apple watch face and keep them top of mind throughout your day. It's the first watch that watches out for you.

ECG on your wrist.

Anytime, anyplace. With the ECG app, Apple Watch Series 5 is proficient in generating an ECG similar to a single-lead electrocardiogram. It's a significant achievement for a wearable device that can provide critical data for doctors and peace of mind for you.

Your finger can tell you much about your heart. Electrodes built into the Digital Crown and the back crystal work together with the ECG app to read the heart's electrical signals. Just touch the Digital Crown to generate an ECG waveform in only 30 seconds. The ECG app can specify if your heart rhythm shows signs of atrial fibrillation. — a severe type of irregular heart rhythm — or normal sinus rhythm, which means your heart is beating in a healthy and regular pattern.

How to use the ECG app

Unusually high or low heart rates and irregular heart rhythms (known as *arrhythmias) could be signs of a severe life-threatening condition. But several people don't recognize the symptoms, so the*

Underlying causes often go undiagnosed. With notifications in the Heart Rate app, Apple Watch Series 5 can check your heart rate. And urgently alert you to these irregularities — so that you can take action and consult your doctor.

Track your cycle with a tap.

The Cycle Tracking App gives you an insight into your menstrual cycle. It can help provide a clearer image of your overall health. In addition to merely confirming that you're preparing, you'll have extra information to help you track any irregularities and symptoms and improve discussions with your doctor.

Safe from the sound.

Environment noise can rise to levels that may affect your hearing without your even realizing it. The new Noise app senses when the roar of the watching crowd or the rumble of machinery reaches a level that may stance a risk. So you can step away or plug up to give your ears a needed break.

Take a breather.

Taking minutes throughout the day to stop, relax, and practice mindfulness can help reduce stress and improve overall mental and physical health. The Breathe app keeps you centered by leading you through a succession of calming breaths. It's available on Apple watch face, so you can bring back focus to your day only by raising your wrist.

Apps that make better health.

The right watch apps can play an important role in prompting you to keep up with healthy routines. Whether you need to manage a condition like diabetes, make healthier food choices, or reduce stress, there's an app designed to help you prioritize your goal. And now that the decent App Store is right on your wrist, it's even easier to find great health apps with your watch.

Dexcom G6 Mobile. If you are managing type 1 or type 2 diabetes, you can now check your glucose levels at-a-glance with this App.

YAZIO. This App can help to log your meals quickly, calculate calories, and track your activity for your diet menu plan.

Meditopia. It can also help you slow down with on the go mediations so that to reduce stress, improve sleep, and find more happiness.

Apple Watch fall detection

Apple Watch Series 5 can quickly detect that you've fallen. When an incident like this happens, a hard fall alert is delivered, and you can initiate a call to emergency services or dismiss the alert. If you're unresponsive after 60 seconds, the emergency call will place automatically. Your emergency contacts list will then be contacted, notified, and sent your location.

International emergency calling.

Now with Apple Watch Series 5, you can complete a call to emergency services anywhere in the world. To do this, just press and hold the side button on Apple Watch Series 5 with Cellular and you'll connect with the help you need. It can works even if you're nowhere near your iPhone.

CHAPTER 3

The ultimate Workout Companion never rests.

Whether you're an athlete or you want to track your daily activity, Apple Watch Series 5 supports you train smarter to get results faster. Now with a display that's continuously on, your metrics are always visible, so you may never have to stop and raise your wrist to see how you're doing. And with more than 50 million songs to stream from Apple Music, you've acquired all the motivation you need to keep moving.

Workouts that don't quit.

When Cycling, yoga, swimming, high-intensity interval training. Just name it, Apple Watch Series 5 measures it. Set your workout-specific goals, then see full summaries when you finish and track how you're trending over time in the Activity app on your iPhone. Apple Watch 5 works for wheelchair users, with two different specific wheelchair workouts.

Don't stop what you're doing to see how it's going. The Workout app has improved for the new display. Whether you're holding a pose or swimming some laps, your metrics are always visible, every distressing second. You're welcome.

Swimming metrics

Strokes of intellect. Apple watch has Water resistant to 50 meters, and Apple Watch Series 5 is well designed with swimmers in mind. The Pool Swim workout records splits and sets and can really recognize your stroke. The Open Water Swim workout visualizes your route on a map.

Running metrics that is a long

Apple Watch Series 5 is made to take the most progressive runner further. Pace alerts give you a gentle tap on the wrist to allow you know if you're behind or ahead of where you like to be. Cadence allows you to see your steps per minute and helps you perfect your running technique. And rolling pace continually updates, allowing you to see your split for the preceding mile at all times.

Knowing exactly where you stand

In addition to counting flights of stairs and providing elevation gain in an outdoor workout, Apple Watch Series 5 gives you your current elevation. So whether you're climbing a hill or descending into a canyon, you know just how high or low you are.

Connected with gym

With just a tap, you can pair your watch with available and compatible gym equipment. So you can keep all essential metrics like heart rate, speed, and calories in sync among your watch and the treadmill, stair climber, you're on.

Plays with others

Apple Watch is the world's largest app store on your wrist, and there's a third-party app for all kinds of methods to round out your exercise routine.

Wikiloc. This App lets you discover millions of outdoor trails around the globe. Pick between hiking, running, MTB, skiing, etc.

Redpoint. This track any climbing and rock sessions, and get detailed feedback on your ascents like the duration, difficulty of the route, and ascending speed.

Group. You can get an in-depth summary of your stand-up-paddling workout, including duration, distance speed, paddle strokes, and heart rate.

Apple watch music

When you get lost in your music, podcasts, or audiobooks. With Apple watch Music on your wrist, you've access more than 50 million tracks of musical motivation to keep you entertained. You can catch up on the most recent podcasts or listen to an audiobook. Stream everything you want right from your watch, even if your phone not within reach.

Activity ring

There are three rings. Appreciating all the ways you move throughout the day is an integral part of living a healthy life.

Apple Watch Series 5 shows your daily movement as three simple metrics:

- *Move*
- *Exercise*
- *Stand.*

These above three make up the Activity rings that track your progress all day long. Apple Watch 5 doesn't just show you how you're doing it but also retains you going with motivation from personal coaching, awards, and Activity Competitions. It's everything you need to stay fired up to near your rings 365.

How to close your Activity rings

Move. The Move ring tracks the active calories you burn. Active calories are the ones you burn through all types of movement, from taking the stairs at work to playing with your kids.

Exercise. The Exercise ring displays you how long minutes of brisk activity you've done, or instead of working out or just moving at a fast pace.

Stand. Sitting too much can give rise to health problems over time. So Apple Watch Series 5 keeps you motivated to get ambulated throughout the day.

Apple Watch Series 5 connectivity

To make phone calls, to texts, to emergency assistance around the world, Apple Watch Series 5 built with Cellular that lets you leave your phone behind and still stay connected. Now that the screen display is always on, your vital information remains front and center.

The freedom of Cellular. Built-in Cellular that allows you go with just your watch. Field a call from the office, text a thumbs-up to a buddy, check your email — the new beast keeps you connected, even without your phone.

Listen up

With the new Audiobooks app on Apple watch series 5, type Apple Books titles in your Reading Now list are automatically syncs to your Apple watch. Apple Watch makes it easier to stream all your favorite events from Apple Podcasts, an album or playlist from Apple Music, or live radio from stations around the world.

Easy money.

Using Apple pay in now comfortable with series 5, double-click the side button and hold your watch to the checkout reader to use Apple Pay

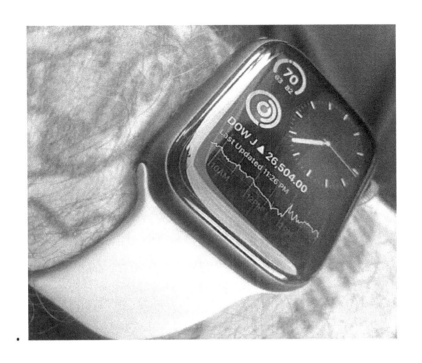

You can send or receive Apple Cash with the Messages app. Apple Pay keeps your financial information entirely private and secure.

CHAPTER 4

Apple Watch buying guide and tips

*A*pple and Fitbit to traditional watchmakers like Tag Heuer and Fossil, many companies are creating smartwatches that bring notifications, apps, and more to your wrist. Even though features and designs vary, smartwatches can help save you time and keep better tabs on your health.

A lot of smartwatches have built-in fitness features, such as a heart rate sensor and GPS. The, for instance, is marketed as a health-focused device rather than a smartphone replacement.

Some smartwatches, even work independently of a phone, but most are design as your companion devices. How do you decide which smartwatch is right for your wishes and budget? Here's a quick guide.

Quick Tips:

If you're interested in one, here are the most important things to consider before you buy any smartwatch:

1. Don't ever buy a smartwatch without confirming that it will work with your Smartphone. For instance, Apple Watches only work with their iPhones. However, other brands like Google's Wear OS platform and Samsung's Tizen watches will work with both Android phones and iPhones. But with

fewer features than if you use them with an Android device.

2. Select a watch with a heart rate sensor and GPS (to track your runs) if you're a fitness buff.

Always pay attention to rated battery life when shopping. Hybrid watches that look more like analog timepieces tend to have the most extended battery life, but they hardly have touch screens.

Ensure that the watch band's clasp or buckle is easy to use and easy to swap. Besides, make sure that it's easy for you to find the replacement of the watch bands.

The selection of apps is another important factor, but it's not as significant as compatibility, design, and other features.

The Device Compatibility

Because most apple watches are designed to serve as companions to your Smartphone, device compatibility is very imperative. For example, Samsung's Tizan power work with numerous Android handsets as well as iPhones, but it's easier to use those watches with an Android device (and precisely a Samsung one).

The Fitbit Versa also works just as well with Android phones as it does with iPhones. But, Android phone owners do get one extra feature that they may quick reply to incoming text messages.

Google's Wear OS watch operating system runs on watches from LG, Huawei, and others and works with Android 4.3 and higher smartphones. If you want to check whether your Smartphone is compatible with Google: go to from your smartphone browser. Some Wear OS watches will work with the iPhone. Still, lots of features (such as adding apps and connecting the watch directly to Wi-Fi) aren't accessible when the clock is linked to iOS devices.

Android Wear 2.0, which rolled out in 2017, brought a slew of new features to watches. Including advanced fitness-tracking features, support for Google Assistant, and the capability to install apps directly on the watch itself. Google rebranded its smartwatch from Android Wear to Wear OS in March 2018 to reflect its cross-platform compatibility. All that you need to do is download the Wear OS app to connect the watch to a smartphone.

Not miraculously, the only works with the iPhone. The preinstalled Apple Watch app for the iPhone is where you'll find the watchOS App Store. There, you can install the watch versions of your favorite iOS apps or find new ones.

The store features all from games to fitness-tracking apps to extensions of your most-used productivity apps so you can get Slack notifications.

Don't buy any watch unless you know that it will work with your Smartphone.

Almost all smartwatches now obtainable with use a colorful LCD screen or AMOLED display, which allows you view photos, apps, and other content in more vibrant color and tend to be brighter. The shortcoming is the shorter battery life, though smartwatch companies are improving the devices' efficiency.

Their color displays use so much power that several watches turn off their screens while they're asleep, so you can't even see the time without waking the device. LCDs tend to be thicker than OLED ones, which is the reasons why Apple developed its first OLED display for the first-generation Apple Watch

On the surface, opting for a touch screen on your Apple watch would seem to be a no-brainer. Still, it can sometimes become challenging to target items on a smaller touch display, and some of the gesture-based interfaces aren't sensitive. Wear OS does an excellent job of presenting card-based notifications you can easily dismiss with a single swipe. Still, there's a lot of swiping concerned to get to other apps and options within apps. The most recent update lets you switch between cards with a flick of your wrist.

With the Apple Watch, Apple opted for a combo approach, presenting a touch display and both a digital crown and side button on the right side. If you like, you can use the crown to zoom in on content quickly or to scroll, and the Apple watch screen uses Force

Touch, which knows the distinction between a tap and a long-press. A press of the side button brings you back to your dock of frequently used apps.

The watch has a bezel that you may rotate to scroll from first to last menus. These are usually used in combination with touch.

Smartwatch Design and Personalization

The better smartwatches give a choice of straps and the ability to swap them out for a third-party option.

It is very important if you want to personalize the look of your device. Most of the watches today offer ample customization options before purchase. For example, you can pick the band color and material, as well as face color, finish, and size for such watches at the same time in case of Apple Watch.

You should keep that in your mind, the comfort counts for a lot, as does the ease with which you can fasten the watch to your wrist. We would avoid any watches with awkward clasps that require too much force to open and close. Fortunately, most new Apple watches use standard buckles.

More and more others watches are sporting round faces now, making them look more like traditional timepieces. Newer ones are getting slimmer, smaller, and smarter.

Alerts and Notifications

Any good watch will alert you to all incoming calls, emails, and text messages with a quick buzz to your wrist, which can help you subtly check whether it's worth answering or not. But you should look for social network integration for notifications from social sites such as Facebook and Twitter.

You must ensure that you'll be able to quickly check all of your most recent notifications, even if you miss them when they first come in. For instance, the Apple Watch lets you swipe down from the top of the screen to see a Notification Center while Wear OS enables you to swipe up from the bottom to see your latest notification.

Some smartwatches out there offer more customization options. The Samsung Gear S3 uses the Gear Manager app on your phone to help you decide which notifications come through to your wrist. There's, also, a Smart Relay feature. Just picking up your phone with the notification displayed on your Gear watch will open the corresponding app on the larger screen.

The Apple Watch allows you to adjust notification settings on the Apple Watch app *for iOS. You can select to mirror the notifications from your iPhone or customize them.*

CHAPTER 5

Apple Watch Series 5 expert review

*T*he Apple Watch Series 5 isn't going to shock you away in the same way as the Apple Watch 4 did – but it does pack one, very important, upgrade over last year's model.

While the iPhone is similar all the time these days. The Apple Watch Series 5 underwent a significant overhaul last year, so not much was expected in terms of improvements this year.

Nevertheless, there has been one significant change: the Apple Watch 5 display doesn't turn off. Its new always-on display allows you to glance down at your Watch - whether that's in a meeting or a workout - and see what's on the screen.

Announced along with the iPhone 11 range at this year's launch event, Apple has confirmed that the Apple Watch 5 release date is Friday, 20 September 2019. That's the same day as the new iPhones.

Series 5 Design and display

Sticking with the same OLED technology that's helped it so well over the years, the Apple Watch 5 comes with a bright and vivid display that's easy to see on your wrist.

Here's the significant change:

Apple has just dropped the 'raise to wake' functionality to see the time or a notification (where you must have to flick or raise your wrist to turn on the display).

We've to impress accuracy earlier line Watches has been at knowing when you're watching on the screen. But now that's all over. You can either see the display in excellent, bright, or the OLED display will massively dim, and you'll be able to see all your key information.

In our tests with it, it was undoubtedly a useful skill for the watch to gain. Of specific benefit was the fact it works in the Workout app, as you can now see what's on the screen without having to flick the wrist.

In a strength workout or fast run, you don't need that extra hassle - and it's great to see Apple drop it. But, it's not clear how this will work with third-party apps, so we'll need to try that out in our detail review.

But at of viewing any angles, in particular, are very impressive when the Watch 5 is dim. You can see it from pretty much any way you want to squint at it, and that's something needed and remarkable.

The larger 40mm and 44mm designs for last year's Apple Watch Series 4 remains, which again is expect for a couple of reasons. Firstly, Apple keeps related designs for years when repeating on its products. Otherwise, it would mean even more sizes of bands and accessories on the market.

Keeping things simple makes the third-party market more exciting and mature, so there's a divine purpose to retain the large 44mm and 40mm models.

The design of the Apple Watch 5 is as most would expect.

Rounded edges with the small speaker grilles in (which, remember, can speak to you and tell you lap or split times as you run around). As well as water resistance up to 5ATM pressure - so swimming with this watch is cool.

The biggest change design-wise in the materials used - Apple has shown the Watch 5 in new ceramic and titanium variants (although the former has used in older models). In a bid to surge the range of price points, it can sell its smartwatch.

These feel good on the wrist, although we weren't impressed with the ceramic option when it first came out. Well, possibly, we could rephrase that - it felt premium for sure, but it didn't quite feel worth the extra cash Apple was requesting for it.

But then again, we're not the target market of bling that this device is aiming for dummies. Even though the cost of the titanium model is a little steep, present the Apple Watch in a new material might, again, entice the upgrade.

There's not much difference at all between the Apple Watch Series 4 and Series 5 - this is just an update to that model. However, the large display and rounded edges still feel elegant on the wrist. And the burgeoning range of bands (not only from Apple) makes it a decent choice for iPhone owners.

Apple hasn't significantly added in the way of fitness capability with the new Watch Series 5, thanks to there not being a vast amount of new hardware to work.

The ECG monitor also remains, but that was the headline of last year, and it's beginning to get medical authorization in many countries now.

The much-vaunted sleep tracking didn't arrive, which makes sense when the battery life hasn't improved. Still, you'll be able to track the full range of fitness options (from running to swimming) from the watch - as well as track your output on gym equipment like steppers or treadmills, etc.

The chipset in Series 4 is called the Apple S4, supported with 16GB of storage capacity for apps or music. Battery life was 18 hours, according to Apple, which looked accurate enough in our year of use: we've been able to eke two days out of our 44mm without too much effort.

On the other hand, the Apple Watch Series 5 gets a 64-bit, dual-core S5 processor (the capacity of storage hasn't announced). Once again, Apple has claimed 18 hours of battery life. It's managed to achieve that without the always-on display using up the battery life.

Thanks to new power administration and the excitingly-named Low-Temperature Polycrystalline Oxide (LTPO) display, a modified of OLED that's much more energy-

efficient than the OLED used in the Apple Watch Series 4. This tech did exist in Series 4, but the wearable wasn't programmed to make the most of it.

LTPO uses a smaller amount of energy to keep the screen updated, and it's particularly useful at lower refresh rates. During the keynote, that it can also move effortlessly from refresh rates as high as 60Hz to a positively sloth-like 1Hz, depending on what you need.

Takeaway

Apple had "always-on," which has been the very top of our wish list since the very first generation. The Apple Watch Series 4 is much quicker to turn on than any prior Apple Watch display. But having to wake up our watch still upsets us, and makes it almost impossible to check the time sneakily when we're bored in meetings. For that feature *alone, we'd agree the Apple Watch Series 5 is better than the Series 4.*

But there's more to the Apple Watch 5 than just the display, as abundant as that is. The compass makes any navigation – land, sea, or air – that little better. There's a broader choice of materials and colors, even if some of them are so amusingly expensive, which most of us won't even glance at their section of the Apple Store. And it's going to be that little bit smoother thanks to its S5 processor.

CHAPTER 6

Apple Watch 5 release date and price

We witnessed the 10 September event, Apple Watch 5 will launch, but we can make an educated guess. It's worthwhile buying the Apple Watch 5 right now as the device is only a couple of weeks old, and we expect to release

from the Apple company pending 20 September 2019.

Apple watch 5

Generally speaking, the Apple Watch 3 and Apple Watch 4 are both introduced in September of their respective years. So the company did follow a similar costume for its Apple Watch Series 5 device.

Regularly Apple introduces devices and then releases them ten days later as well, so this version will also be available after ten days of the great event.

Outstanding handling and safety information about Apple watch

My dear, you should take the necessary precautions to protect. Failure to follow this safety information could result in fire, electric shock, injury, or damage to your Apple watch or other property. Take time and read all the safety information in this chapter before using your new Apple Watch Series 5.

Ways to handle Apple Watch.

The Apple Watch cover case made up of various materials. That includes Apple Watch 316L stainless steel, ceramic, and sapphire crystal. The Apple Watch Sport

7000 series has aluminum, Ion-X glass that is strengthened glass, plastics.

It is made up of 18karat gold, sapphire crystal, ceramic Apple Watch contains sensitive electronic machinery, and can be spoiled if dropped, burned, punctured, or crushed. However, you should not use any damaged Apple Watch. Such as one with a cracked screen, visible water intrusion, a damaged band, because it may cause injury. Keep it away from heavy exposure to dust or sand.

Repairing Apple Watch

Don't ever open the Apple Watch, and don't try to fix Apple Watch yourself. The reasons are that disassembling Apple Watch may perhaps damage it, result in failure of water resistance, and may cause injury to you as well. If Apple Watch is malfunctioning or damaged, contact an Apple Authorized Service Provider.

Don't try to replace the Apple Watch battery by yourself. You may probably damage the battery, which could cause overheating and subsequent injury. The lithium-ion battery in Apple smart Watch should be serviced only by an authorized qualified service provider. You could receive a replacement Apple Watch when ordering battery service. Batteries must be recycled and appropriately disposed of separately of household waste. You should never incinerate the battery.

Distraction sometimes may occur using Apple Watch. In some circumstances may cause a dangerous situation (for instance, avoid texting while driving your car or using headphones while riding a bicycle).

Observe all rules that prohibit or restrict the use of mobile phones or headphones (But you may allow using hands-free options for making calls while driving).

Maps Navigation

Apple watches series five built- with GPS capability Maps, directions, and location-based apps depend on data services. These data services are subject to change from time to time. They may not be obtainable in all areas, resulting in maps, directions, or location-based instructions that may be unavailable, inaccurate, or incomplete. Some map features require your Location Services. Always compare the information provided by Apple Watch to your environs and defer to posted signs to resolve any discrepancies. Do not use these services while doing activities that need your full attention. For all time, comply with posted road signs and the laws and regulations in the areas where you are using Apple Watch and at all the times use your common sense.

How to charge Apple Watch

To charge Apple Watch, use only the Apple Watch Magnetic charging cable, and it is the power adapter. For Apple Watch Edition, the included Apple Watch Magnetic. You may likely use third-party Lightning cables with 5W power adapters featuring an MFi logo. It's imperative to keep Apple Watch, the Apple Watch Magnetic charging cable, and the power adapter in a dry, well-ventilated area when charging. When charging Apple smart Watch Edition in the Apple Watch Magnetic charging case, always keep the case open. Using an Apple Watch damage Magnetic charging cable or charging case when moisture is present, can cause fire, spark, electric shock. Which may result in injury or damage to Apple Watch or other property.

Ensure that, Apple Watch and the Apple Watch Magnetic charging cable or Apple Watch Magnetic charging case are well dry before charging whenever you use the Apple Watch Magnetic charging cable or Apple Watch Magnetic charging case to charge Apple watch. Make sure that your USB plug inserted fully into the adapter before you plug the adapter into a power outlet.

You should avoid charging Apple Watch in direct sunlight. Moreover, remember; don't wear your smartwatch while it is charging.

Lightning cable and connector

Lightning cable and connector should avoid prolonged skin contact. With the connector when the Lightning to USB cable is plugged into a power source because it may cause *irritation or injury. Sleeping or sitting on the Lightning connector should be avoided.*

Prolonged heat exposure to Apple Watch.

The Apple smartwatch Magnetic charging cable, the Apple Watch magnetic charging case, and the power adapter complies with appropriate surface-temperature standards and limits. Still, even within these limits, sustained contact with warm surfaces for extended periods may cause soreness or injury. Apple Smartwatch and magnetic charging cable, the Apple Watch Magnetic charging case, and the power adapter will become very warm when plugged into a power source. Use universal precaution to avoid situations where your skin is in prolonged contact with Apple Watch. The Apple Watch magnetic charging cable, the Apple Watch magnetic charging case, or the power adapter for long periods when they're plugged in. For instance, while

Apples Watch is charging or the Apple Watch magnetic charging cable, or Magnetic charging case. The power adapter is plugged into a power outlet so that you don't sleep on them or place them under a blanket, pillow, or your body. Take extraordinary care if you have any physical condition that affects your ability to detect heat against the body. Always remove Apple smart Watch if it becomes disturbingly warm.

Listening sound at high volume

Hearing loss may result when Listening to sound at high volumes may damage your hearing. Background noise, as well as constant exposure to high volume levels, can make sounds seem quieter than they are. Usually, turn on audio playback and make sure the volume level before inserting a Bluetooth connected headset in your ear is within the safety level. To prevent potential *hearing damage, do not listen to high volume levels for Radiofrequency exposure. Apple Smart Watch uses radio signals to connect to wireless networks.*

Radiofrequency interference

You should also observe the signs and notices that prohibit or restrict the use of electronic devices (for example, in healthcare facilities or blasting areas). Even though Apple smart Watch, the Apple Watch magnetic charging cable, and the Apple Watch magnetic charging case are better designed. Tested, and manufactured to comply with regulations governing radio frequency emissions, so all emissions from Apple Watch. The Apple Watch magnetic charging cable and the Apple Watch magnetic charging case can negatively affect the function of another electronic gadget, causing them to malfunction. The best thing to do is to unplug the Apple

Watch magnetic charging cable. As well as the Apple Watch magnetic charging case. Turn off Apple Watch or use the Airplane mode when the use of Apple Watch is prohibited, like when traveling in aircraft, or when asked to do so by state authorities.

Medical device interference

Apple smart Watch contains components and radios that emit electromagnetic waves. Apple Watch, some of the bands, the Apple Watch magnetic charging cable, and the Apple Watch magnetic charging case enclose magnets. These electromagnetic waves and magnets may impede with pacemakers, defibrillators, and other medical devices.

Always maintain a safe distance of parting between your medical device and Apple Watch, its bands, the Apple smart Watch magnetic charging cable, and the Apple Watch magnetic charging case.

The most important thing is to consult your physician and medical device company for information specific to your medical device. Stop using Apple Watch when its bands or the Apple Watch magnetic charging cable, and the Apple Watch magnetic charging case. If you expect, they are interfering with your pacemaker, hearing aids, defibrillator, or any other medical device.

Apple Watch is not a medical device. Still, it has the heart rate sensor, and that's been included Apple Watch apps are not medical devices and are intended for fitness only. They are not designed for use in the clinical diagnosis of a disease or other conditions or the cure, easing treatment, or prevention of medical illness.

Before starting or modifying any physical exercise program using Apple smart Watch, consult your physician. Be cautious and attentive while exercising. Stop exercising if you experience pain or feel faint, dizzy, exhausted, or short of breath.

As a result of exercising, you assume all associated natural risks, including any injury that may result from such activity. If you have any medical condition that you consider could be affected by Apple Watch (for example, seizures, blackouts, eyestrain, and headaches), it's better to consult your physician before using Apple Watch.

Explosive atmospheres device

Charging or using Apple Watch in any area with a potent, tense atmosphere. Such as areas where the air contains high levels of flammable gases, vapors, or particles (like grain, dust, or metal powders), may be hazardous. Comply with all signs and instructions.

Take note of high-consequence activities. Apple Watch is not wished for use where the failure of the device could lead to any loss of life, personal injury, or severe environmental consequences.

Choking hazard, some small Apple Watch bands may present a choking hazard to small children. Keep these bands away from reaching small children.

Skin sensitivity reaction

Some people may experience skin reactions to certain materials used in jewelry, watches, and other wearable items that are in prolonged contact with your skin. It may be due to allergies, environmental factors, exposure, extensive to irritants such as soap, sweat, or other causes.

You may be more liable to experience irritation from any wearable device if you have *allergies and other sensitivities. If you have recognized skin sensitivities, please take special care when wearing Apple Watch. You may be more likely to experience irritation from Apple smart Watch if you wear it too tightly. Strip off Apple Watch periodically to let your skin breathe.*

Keeping smart Watches and the band clean and dry will surely reduce the possibility of skin irritation. If you experience any of redness, swelling, itchiness, or any other irritation sign or discomfort on your skin, or beneath, your Apple Watch, please remove it and consult your physician before resuming wear. Persistent use, even after symptoms subside, may result in an increased irritation.

Nickel hypersensitivity

Apple Smart Watch, particularly, the space gray Apple Watch Sport, the stainless steel portions of some Apple Watch bands, and the magnets in the watch and groups have some nickel. Nickel's exposure to these materials is improbable. Still, customers with known nickel hypersensitivity should be attentive when wearing them until when they can determine they are not experiencing an allergic reaction.

Apple Watch, the Milanese Loop, Modern Buckle, and Leather Loop bands comprise of trace amounts of methacrylates from adhesives. Methacrylates usually found in many consumer products that are exposed to the skin, including adhesive bandages. However, some people may be sensitive to them or increase sensitivities over time.

The materials used in Apple Watch and the Apple Watch bands must meet with the standards set in jewelry by the U.S.

Consumer Product Safety Commission, applicable European regulations.

CHAPTER 7

How to get started

Your Apple Watch can respond to your gestures.

*I*f you like to use Apple Watch and its apps, it required these gestures. The Apple Watch display not only responds to touch-based gestures alone, such as tapping and swiping, but also uses (FTT) Force Touch Technology to act in response to the small pressure of your fingertip Tap.

How to set your Watch pair with the iPhone

Toward setup, Watch this book will guide you through a few simple steps to pair Apple Watch with your iPhone and make it customaries to your wish. If you have any difficulty seeing the Apple Watch or iPhone screen to set it set up and pair

Here are the solutions; Update your iPhone to iOS software version 8.2 or much later.

Then, go to Settings> General > Software Update, which includes the travel companion Apple Watch app. After that, open the Apple Watch app on your iPhone.

Put your Apple Watch on your wrist, press and hold the side button until you see the Apple logo displays on the screen.

Once prompted, you should position your iPhone so that Apple Watch appears in the camera viewfinder on your iPhone screen. Strictly follow the orders on iPhone and Apple Watch to ensure the setup finish accurately. It is vital during the setup session; you will select your desired language, your watch orientation, and your passcode.

You may need to charge your device to battery full capacity before pairing it with iPhone so that you will experience any power interruption during the setup session.

For the best performance of your Apple Watch, always change or clean the watch band. Apple Watch should fit closely loosely, but comfortably on your wrist and adjust it accordingly.

The Status icons of you Apple Watch at the top of the screen provide information about Apple smart Watch:

1. Notification: You have unread notifications.

2. Charging: Apple Watch is charging.

3. Lock: Apple Watch is a lock with a passcode.

4. Do Not Disturb: Calls and alerts won't sound or light up the screen, but alarms are still in effect.

5. Airplane Mode: Wireless is turned off, but non-wireless features are still available.

6. Apple watch disconnected from your iPhone: Apple Watch has lost the connection with its paired iPhone.

7.Loading: A wireless activity or an active process is happening.

The Apple Watch app on iPhone

The Watch app on iPhone lets you modify watch settings and options, and you may set up Apple Pay for Apple Watch. It gives you access to the App Store that you can download and install a lot of apps for your Apple smart Watch.

Open your Apple Watch app. Then on iPhone, tap the Apple Watch application *icon, tap My Watch to open the settings for Apple smart Watch.*

Power on, wake, and unlock

When your Apple Watch is off, press and hold the side button on your Watch until the Apple logo displays, and you might see a black screen appear for a short time, at that moment waiting for the watch face.

Turn off Apple smart Watch.

You will be able to power off Apple Watch—then press and hold the side button until the slider display, then drag it to the right of your watch.

Wake Apple Watch.

If you want to wake up, Apple smart, lift, or raised your wrist or tap on display. And your Apple Watch goes to sleep when you lower your wrist. You can as well wake Apple smart Watch by pressing the Digital Crown that is useful if you're not on your wrist.

But if Apple smart Watch doesn't wake when you lift your wrist, now you must ensure that you've selected the right wrist and Digital Crown orientation.

Open the Settings app on your watch and make sure you're looking at the watch face. Then press the Digital Crown to get to the Home screen, tap, go to General > Orientation.

Then ensure that Orientation set to the wrist you wear Apple Watch.

You can set Apple smart Watch to give you an idea about the watch face when it wakes up, or return to where you were before it went to sleep. The default setting is to wake the watch face.

Select return back to the last app you used

Open Settings on your smart Watch, tap General >Activate on Wrist Raise, and make Wrist Raise is turn on.

Then scroll down to select opening to the last-used app. You might also do this through the Apple Watch app on iPhone:

Tap My Watch, go to General > Activate on Wrist Raise, then choose Resume Previous Activity.

Unlock Apple Watch with iPhone.

You can unlock your Apple smart Watch by putting your iPhone passcode on iPhone, open the Apple smart Watch app on iPhone, tap My Watch, tap Passcode, then tap Unlock with iPhone. Or, on Apple Watch, open Settings, scroll down, tap Passcode, then turn on Unlock with iPhone.

Remember that you can set up Your Apple Watch passcode to differ from your iPhone passcode. In fact, for more security of your gadgets, it is better to make the passcodes different.

How to enter a passcode into Apple Watch

Whenever you take Apple smart Watch off your wrist or wear it very slackly, it always asks for your passcode the next time you try to use it. When the number pad displays, tap your passcode.

To change your passcode

On Apple smart Watch, open Settings, scroll down, tap Passcode, then tap Change Passcode and follow the on-screen step prompts. Enter the at least a new 4-digit passcode, then confirm it. Alternatively, open the Apple smart Watch app on iPhone, tap My Watch, tap Passcode, then tap Change Passcode and follow the onscreen prompts.

How to change the passcode

Enter a longer passcode.

If you wish to use a passcode longer than four digits, open the Apple Watch app on iPhone, tap My Watch, tap Passcode, then turn off Simple Passcode. A simple passcode is a four-digit number. With this option, you can set more than four-digit passcode on your Apple smart Watch.

To turn off the passcode

Open Settings, tap Passcode and then tap Disable Passcode. Alternatively, open the Apple smart Watch app on iPhone, tap My Watch, tap Passcode, and then tap Turn Passcode Off. Mind you. If you ever Disable your passcode, you can no longer use Apple Pay on Apple smart Watch.

You can lock it automatically.

Turn on wrist recognition as a detection to lock your watch automatically when you're not wearing it. Open the Apple smart Watch app on iPhone, tap My Watch, tap General, and then tap Wrist Detection. When you turn on Wrist Detection, you can also see the time when you raise your wrist. If you turn off

Wrist Detection, you cannot even use Apple Pay.

You can lock it manually.

Here you Press and hold the side button until the display of the slider, then yank the Lock Device slider to the right. You'll be asked to enter your Watch passcode the next time you try to use Apple Watch. You can also put the watch into Power Reserve mode from the screen.

How to erase Apple Watch data

You may set Apple Watch to erase its data if the wrong password is entered ten times. it protects the contents of your watch if it is stolen or lost.

Open the Apple smart Watch app on iPhone, tap My Watch, tap Passcode, and then tap Erase Data.

But If you fail to remember your passcode, what to do?

Unpaired Apple Watch from its paired iPhone. To delete your Apple Watch settings and passcode. You may also reset Apple Watch and pair it once again with your iPhone.

How to adjust brightness, text size, sounds, and haptics

To adjust brightness. On the watch Settings app, then scroll down and tap Brightness & Text Size.

Tap a Brightness icon, then turn the Digital Crown or tap the brightness icon to adjust. Alternatively, open the Apple Watch app on iPhone, tap My Watch, tap Brightness and Text Size, and then drag the Brightness slider.

Compose the text larger.

Open smart Watch Settings, then scroll down and tap Brightness & Text Size. Tap Text Size, then tap the letters or scroll the Digital Crown to enlarge or reduce the text size. Alternatively, open the Apple smart Watch app on iPhone, tap My Watch, tap Brightness & Text Size, and pull the Text Size slider.

How to make the text bold

On your smartwatch, Settings, scroll down and tap Brightness and Text Size. Click on Bold Text. Alternatively, open the Apple smart Watch app on iPhone, tap My Watch, tap Brightness & Text Size, and then turn on Bold Text.

Whenever you turn on bold text from any of Apple Watch or your paired iPhone, Apple

Watch has to be reset to apply the change. Then tap Continue.

How to adjust Apple Watch sound

Open your smart Watch Settings, then scroll down and tap Sounds and Haptics. Tap the volume buttons below Ringer and Alert Sounds or tap the slider one time to select it, and then turn the Digital Crown to regulate the volume. Alternatively, open the Apple smart Watch app on iPhone, tap My Watch, tap Sounds & Haptics, then pull the Ringer and Alert Sounds slider.

Mute Apple smart Watch.

To mute, you watch just open Settings, and scroll down and tap Sounds and Haptics, then turn on Mute. Or otherwise, swipe up on the watch face, Swipe to the Settings glance, then tap the Mute button. You may also open the Apple Watch app on iPhone, tap My Watch, tap Sounds and Haptics, then turn on Mute. Apple Watch connected to its companion iPhone.

Turn on Mute.

You can swiftly mute new alerts and all notification sounds by resting the palm of your hand on the watch display and holding it there for at least four seconds. You'll be aware of a tap to confirm that mute is on. You must initially turn on the option in the Apple Watch app on iPhone. Then tap My Watch, tap Sounds and Haptics, turn on Cover to Mute.

How to adjust the haptic intensity

On your Apple smart Watch, taps your wrist for certain notifications and alerts, and you can regulate the strength of these haptics. Open Settings, then scroll down and tap Sounds & Haptics. Tap the haptic buttons below Ringer and Alert Haptics or tap the slider once to choose it, then turn the Digital Crown to adjust the haptic intensity. Alternatively, open the Apple Watch app on iPhone, tap My Watch, tap Sounds & Haptics, then pull the Ringer and Alert Haptics slider.

Do Not Disturb is a simple way to silence Apple's SmartWatch.

It keeps calls and alerts except for alarms from making any sounds or lighting up the screen.

How to turn on Do Not Disturb

Swipe up on the smartwatch face, swipe left, or right to the Settings peek, then tap the Do Not Disturb button. Or open Settings, tap Do Not Disturb, then turn on Do Not Disturb. Whenever Do Not Disturb is on, you'll see them at the top of the screen. Tap to turn on Do Not Disturb.

To silence, both Apple Watch and iPhone

Open the Apple Watch app on iPhone, tap My Watch, and turn on Do Not Disturb > Mirror iPhone. Moreover, any time you can change Do Not Disturb on one, the other will change to match.

How to modify Apple Watch language and orientation

If you want to change the language or your region format. Then unlock the Apple Watch app on your iPhone, tap on My Watch, then go to General > Language and Region.

Control wrists or modify the Digital Crown orientation.

If you would like to switch wrists or instead to orient the Digital Crown another way, adjust the orientation settings so that when raising your wrist will wake Apple Watch, and turning the Digital Crown moves things in the direction you look forward.

Now open the Settings app, then go to General > Orientation. To change the settings in the Apple smart Watch app on iPhone, then tap My Watch, then go to General> Watch Orientation.

Set orientation options on Apple Watch or in the Apple Watch app.

How to charge your Apple Watch

Make sure that you always charge Apple smart Watch. In a well-ventilated place. Position the built-in Apple Watch magnetic charging cable or Apple Watch magnetic charging case on a flat surface. Then plug it into the included power adapter in the Apple Watch pack, or you may even use a power adapter. You can use it with your iPhone or iPad and then plug it into an appropriate power outlet. Once using the Apple Watch magnetic charging case, always keep the case open.

Place and position the back of Apple Watch on your charger. In such a way that the magnets on the charger line up Apple Watch properly, and you'll hear a chime sound except if the Apple Watch is muted mode and see a charging sign on your watch face. The charging flag is red when Apple smart Watch wants power and turns green when Apple smart Watch is charging.

Checking battery power remaining

On Apple smart Watch, swipes up on the watch face, then swipe to the battery glance. You can add the battery indicator to several of the watch faces, plus modular, color, utility, simple, chronograph, and Mickey mouse. With the watch face showing, firmly press the display, tap, customize, and then swipe to the left until you can select individual feature locations. Here tap a place, turn the Digital

Crown to choose a battery, and then press the Digital Crown to exit.

You can set Apple smart Watch in power reserve mode so that to save power when the battery is low. Apple smart Watch continues to keep and display time, but other apps will not be available for use. Swipe up on your watch face, swipe to the power glance, tap power reserve, then tap Proceed. You may also press the side button until you see the slide show, and then drag it to the right.

You should take note that, your Apple smart Watch can automatically enters into power reserve mode if the percentage your battery charge left behind drops below 10 percent.

How to return to normal power mode

Just press and hold the side button to restart Apple smart Watch. Make sure there is *sufficient charge in the battery for this to work correctly.*

Checking time for the last charge

Open the Apple smart Watch app on iPhone, tap My Watch, then go to General> Usage, where you can outlook the Usage and Standby values. These values, further together, give you the elapsed time since your last full charge. Below that, you can see the power reserve value.

CHAPTER 8

How to organize apps

*T*hey're all on a single Home screen, where you can hold them as you wish. To open an app, your smartwatch. On your watch face, press the Digital Crown to get to the Home screen, and then tap the app icon. Alternatively, turn the Digital Crown to open either app is in the center of your Watch Home screen.*

To return to the last apps is to click the Digital Crown double.

To return to the watch face

Tap the watch icon on the Home screen to respond to your watch face. Alternatively, press the Digital Crown.

Rearrange your apps.

On your Apple smart Watch, press the Digital Crown to go to the watch home screen.

Touch and hold an app till the apps shake to and fro, and the app icons appear the same size and then drag the app you want to move to a new place. Press the Digital Crown when you've done it. Alternatively, open the Apple smart Watch app on iPhone, tap My Watch, then tap App Layout. Touch and hold an app symbol, then drag it to a new place. Tap Reset to restore the original layout setting.

How to get and install apps from the App Store

Open the Apple smart Watch app on iPhone, and then tap the App Store to find apps for your Apple Smart Watch. Buy it, download, and install apps on your iPhone. On your Apple Smart Watch, you'll notice a message prompting you asking to install the app. Then tap Yes.

Open the Apple smart Watch app on your iPhone, tap My Watch, and scroll down to see your apps you want to improve. Tap an app name to change its settings.

To check storage used by apps

Open the Apple smart Watch app on your iPhone, tap My Watch, then go to General > Usage. View the room used by each app and the accessible storage left on Apple smart Watch.

On your Watch home screen, touch and hold the app icon until you view an X on the border. Then tap the X to get rid of the app from Apple smart Watch. It remains installed on your paired iPhone, unless if you remove it from there.

To display or hide installed apps

On your Apple smartwatch, open the Apple smart Watch app on iPhone, tap My Watch, scroll down to view apps you've already installed, tap the app name, and then tap Show App on Apple smart Watch. However, mind you, you cannot hide any apps that already in-build with your Apple Smart Watch.

How to get in touch with your friends

The side button on your Apple smartwatch gives you swift access to people you live in touch with the most. Press the side button, choose a friend, then call, send a message, or use Digital Touch. Add your friends to your Apple Watch.

How to add friends to Apple smartwatch on iPhone

Apple Watch routinely adds up to 12 of your choice contacts from the iPhone. You can amend the list of friends that appear on your Apple smartwatch, open the Apple Watch app, then tap My Watch, then tap Friends. In your friend's list, tap Add friend, then tap your friend in the list of contacts that appears o the screen. If your friend's name isn't on the list, open the Contacts app on your iPhone and add them, subsequently try again.

To see friends on Apple smart Watch

Press the side button to see up to 12 friends' contact. Turn the Digital Crown to highlight every one of your friends. Tap a friend's initials, and then select how you want to get in touch.

How to use Hand to shift between Apple Watch and iPhone

The Hand of aspect on Apple Watch and iPhone lets you move from one device to another without losing focus on what you're doing. For instance, you can check email on Apple smart Watch, but you may want to switch to iPhone to type an answer using the on-screen keyboard. Wake iPhone, and you see a symbol in the lower-left corner of the Lock screen that matches the app you're using on Apple smart Watch-for instance, Mail. Swipe up on the sign to open the same email on the iPhone, and then finish your reply.

You may use Handoff with these apps: Mail, Maps, Messages, Phone, Calendar, and Remember as well as Siri. For Handoff to work, your Apple smart Watch should be close to your iPhone.

How to turn Handoff

Open the Apple smart Watch app on your iPhone, then tap My Watch, then turn on General> Enable Handoff.

How to locate your iPhone

Misplaced your iPhone? Apple Watch can help you find out if it's nearby. Ping your iPhone.

Swipe up on a watch face, swipe to the Settings glance, tap the Ping iPhone button.

If the iPhone is not in the range of Apple Smart Watch, you can also try to find it using Find My iPhone from the site called iCloud.com.

How to use your watch without pairing with iPhone

Even though you need an iPhone to do most of the things with your smart Watch, but you can still do quite many things with Apple Watch without having an iPhone in range.

You can do the following without pairing with your iPhone

1. To play music from a stored playlist on Apple Watch

2. To use the watch, alarms, timers, and its stopwatch

3. You can keep a trail of your activity such as stand, move, and exercise with the Activity app in the smart Watch

4. You can also track your workouts

5. To display photos from stored photo albums

6. To use Apple Pay to make purchases in an online store.

Apple Smart Watch uses Bluetooth wireless technology to bond to its paired iPhone. It uses the iPhone for several wireless functions. Apple smartwatch can't connect with new WiFi networks by itself, although it can connect to WiFi networks you've already set up on the iPhone.

If Apple smart Watch and iPhone are on the same network ranges but are not connected by Bluetooth, you can do the following on Apple Watch with no iPhone:

1. You can send and receive messages using iMessage

2. And you can post and receive Digital Touch messages

3. Using of Siri

The function of Siri on Apple Smart Watch

The Siri on Apple can execute tasks and deliver lots of information right on Apple smart Watch.

How to ask Siri a question

To request an issue to Seri, raise Apple smart Watch or tap on the screen. When the Watch wakes, speak, "Hey, Siri."

You can alternatively press and hold the Digital Crown on the watch. Until you see the listening icon at the bottom of the screen, state your request and then release the Digital Crown. To answer back to a question from Siri and continue the conversation, hold down the Digital Crown and talk. On the other hand, say "Hey, Siri" and your request.

Press and hold to activate Siri.

You'll discover suggestions of things you can ask Siri throughout this book -they look like this:

"What kinds of things can I ask you?"

When you fly with Apple Watch

When you are about to fly an airline, some airlines might let you fly with Apple smart Watch, and iPhone turned on if you put them in Airplane Mode so they can't obstruct with aircraft wave systems.

How to turn on Airplane Mode

To turn on Airplane Mode in your smartwatch. Swipe up on the watch face, and a Settings glance, then tap the Airplane Mode button.

The Connected status of an airplane icon at the top of the screen changes to Disconnected. Or otherwise, open the Settings app, then tap Airplane Mode. When Airplane Mode is on, you'll see it at the top of the screen of your watch.

If you want to set both Apple Watch and iPhone in Airplane Mode, open the Apple Watch app on iPhone, tap My Watch, and turn on Airplane Mode >

Mirror iPhone. Then, at any given time, you switch to Airplane Mode on one gadget, the other will change to match it appropriately.

To turn off *Airplane Mode, you ought to do it for each device separately. However, it is better to turn off Wi-Fi and Bluetooth, but the Apple smart Watch in Airplane Mode.*

CHAPTER 9

How to customize your watch face

You may customize your Apple smart Watch face, so it looks the way you feel like and provides the functions you want.

Select from types of watch face designs, adjust colors, facial appearance, and other details. Then add it to your collection; subsequently, you can switch when you like the right timekeeping tools or when you'd like a change the face.

To change the watch face

With the Apple watch face showing, tightly press the display, and then swipe to see the faces in your collection. When you find the look you want, tap it. Swipe to see other watch faces. Tap to add features to your watch face.

You can add extraordinary functions. Occasionally refers to complications to your watch face, so you can directly check something like stock prices or the weather report.

Add features to your Apple watch face.

On the watch face, firmly press the display, then tap Customize. Swipe to choose a feature, and then turn the Digital Crown to adjust. But on some watch faces, you have to touch an element to pick it.

Then, press the Digital Crown to save your modification. Tap the face to switch to it. Turn the Digital Crown to adjust features.

Ways to add a watch face to the collection.

Gather your collection of custom faces, even different versions of the same design. When your watch face showing, tightly press the display, swipe from to the right, then tap the New button (+). And swipe up and down to select designs, then tap the one you like to add. After you add it, you also can customize it.

How to delete a face from your collection

If you don't like a face much anymore? By the current watch face showing, tightly press the display, swipe to the face that you don't feel like, then swipe it up and tap delete. You can all the time add the watch face again later.

How to increase the watch time ahead.

If you want to set your watch time ahead? Open the Settings app, tap Time, tap +0 min, and then turn the Digital Crown to set the watch ahead to a great extent of 59 minutes. However, this setting can only change the time shown on the Apple watch face even though it doesn't affect alarms, times in notifications, and any other times like World Clock.

Apple's smartwatch consists of a different watch face, some of which you can customize. You should frequently check for software updates, and the set of watch faces that follows might vary from what you see on your Apple smart Watch.

Solar system astronomy of Apple Watch

The Astronomy watch face displays the status of the solar system and the precise position of the planets, sun, and moon. It shows the day, date, and current time zone.

Tap the Moon to see its current phase.

Tap to see the current position of the planets in the solar system. While viewing the Earth, moon, or the solar system, it turns the Digital Crown to move back or forward in time.

Chronograph

This watch face is dealing with time in exact increments, like a classic analog stopwatch. A chronograph is like a stopwatch, which can be activated right from the face.

Apple watches notifications.

The function of this App sends notifications to keep you informed, always such as meeting invitations, messages, and exercise reminders are just a few mentions. Notifications are displayed on Apple Watch as almost immediately as they arrive. If you do not read them instantly away, they can be saved. Thus you can check them later.

How to reply to live notifications

When you get a new notification. If you hear or feel a notification beep arrives, raise Apple smart Watch to view it. Turn the Digital Crown to scroll to the bottom of the notification, and then tap a button there. Alternatively, tap the app symbol in the notification to open the related app.

To dismiss a notification

Swipe down on the notification you're about reading,

or scroll to the bottom of the notification and then tap Dismiss.

How to select which notifications you like

On your iPhone, go to Settings>Notifications to identify which apps and events create notifications. Then, open the Apple smart Watch app on iPhone, tap My Watch, tap Notifications, tap the app for instant, Messages, then select Mirror my iPhone. or, to choose different notification settings than those on iPhone, select Custom instead

How to silence the notifications

To silence notifications on Apple smart Watch, swipe up on the watch face, swipe to the settings glance, then tap on Silent Mode. You'll feel a tap when a notification arrives. Put off sound or tap, and tap Do Not Disturb.

Keep your Watch private.

You raise your wrist to see a notification; you get a swift summary, then details a few seconds later. For instance, when a message arrives, you know who it's from earlier, and then the message appears. If you want to stop the notification from appearing later completely, you tap it. Open the Apple Smart Watch app on iPhone, tap My Watch, tap Notifications, and then turn on Notification Privacy.

Seeing notifications that haven't responded. If you don't respond to a given notification when it arrives, it's save in Notification Center in your Watch. A red dot at the top of your watch face indicates you have an unread notification. Swipe down on the face to view it. If you want to scroll the notification list, swipe up, down, or turn the Digital Crown.

To respond to a notification in your list. Tap the notification.

Tap a notification to respond to it.

How to clear notifications

Apple smart Watch always removes notifications from the list when you tap to read them. But if you want to delete a notification without understanding it, swipe it to the left, and then tap Clear.

Moreover, if you like to clear all notifications, tightly press the display, and then tap Clear.

CHAPTER 10

Quick glances

*T*o get a quick glance at the valuable information from your watch face, then you have immediate access to Glances, a scannable summary of the data you view mainly. Swipe up on the watch face to see glances, then swipe left or right to see different types of glances. Swipe left or right to view all glimpses.

Check your glances

Swipe up on your watch face to see the glimpse you viewed last, then swipes left or right on your Apple Watch to see other glances. Swipe down to return to the watch face. If a glance isn't enough. To open the related app, tap the glance.

How to organize your glances

To select your glances, open the Apple smartwatch app on iPhone, tap My Watch, tap Glances, and then remove or include glimpses. You can't remove the settings glance totally. But put them in a handy sort. Open your Apple smartwatch app on iPhone, tap My Watch, tap Glances, and then pull the reorder buttons.

The timekeeping appearance of Apple smartwatch, you can see the time in other cities of the world, set alarms, use timers, and use a stopwatch. You can also add these basics to your watch face to see them swiftly when you need them.

How to check the time in other locations

The World Clock app on Apple smart Watch lets you can check the time in cities around the world. Open the app to check times at another place, or add ports to your watch face for swift reference.

For instance, "What time is it now in New York?"

Check the time in a different city.

Open World Clock on your smart Watch, and then turn the Digital Crown or swipe the screen to scroll down the list.

If there is a city location whose time you'd like to see, you can add the world clock to your watch face and select the city name to display.

See Additional Information.

To see more information about a city, together with a time of sunrise and sunset, taps the city in the World Clock list. When you're ending, tap < in the upper left, or swipe right to return to the city list. You can press the

Digital Crown to return to the Apple watch face.

Add any city to the World Clock. The towns you need to add on the iPhone displays in World Clock on Apple smart Watch.

Open the Clock app on iPhone, tap World Clock, and then tap the Add button (+).

Add a world clock to your watch face

You can add a world clock to quite a few watch faces; some faces give permission you add more than one. Tightly press the display, and then tap Customize. Swipe left until you can choose individual facial features, tap the one you'd want to use for a world clock, then turn the Digital Crown to select a city. When you're done, press the Digital Crown. You may add a world clock to these faces:

Such as Chronograph, Color, Mickey Mouse, Modular, Simple, and Utility.

To change city abbreviations. If you like to replace a city abbreviation used on Apple smartwatch, open the Apple Watch app on iPhone, tap My Watch, then go to Clock > City Abbreviations. Tap whichever city to change its abbreviation.

How to set an alarm

To use the Alarm Clock app to play a sound or vibrate Apple smart Watch at the right time. You may also add an alert to your watch face. Thus you can see upcoming alarms at a glimpse. Moreover, open the Alarm Clock app with a tap.

"Set repeating alarm for a PM."

To add an alarm to your Watch. Open Alarm Clock, tightly press the display, then tap New +. Tap Change Time, Tap AM or

PM, *tap the hours or minutes, turn the Digital Crown to change, and then tap Set. Tap < in the upper left to return to the alarm settings, then set repeat, label, and snooze that suit you.*

Add alarm. Set an alarm time. Select options.

Set or adjust your alarm. Open Alarm Clock, then tap the alarm in the list to modify its settings. Tap next to the alarm to turn it on or off. Moreover, tap to edit an alarm.

"Turn off 7:30 alarm."

See the upcoming alarm on the watch face. On the watch face showing, tightly press the display, and then tap Customize. Swipe left until you can choose individual facial features, tap the one you'd like to apply for alarms, and then turn the Digital Crown to select the alarm. When you're finished, press the Digital Crown. You can add alarms to these faces:

Chronograph, Color, Mickey Mouse, Modular, Simple, and Utility.

If you like a snooze, whenever an alarm sounds, you can tap Snooze to wait some minutes before the alarm sounds again. If you do not feel like to allow snooze, tap the alarm in the list of alarms, then turn off Snooze.

To delete an alarm

 Open Alarm Clock, tap the alarm in the list, scroll down to the bottom, and then tap Delete.

How to use a timer

The Timer app on Apple smart Watch can assist you in keeping track of time. Set timers for up to 24 hours.

"Set timer for twenty minutes."

Set a timer. Open Timer, tap hours or minutes, turn the Digital Crown to adjust and then tap Start.

If you want to set a timer for longer than 12 hours, although adjusting the timer, tightly press the display, and then tap 24. So that to increase timer length.

How to Add a timer to watch face

If you want to use a timer frequently, add a timer to your watch face. With the watch face showing, tightly press the display, and then tap Customize. Swipe left until you can select the individual face appearance, tap the one you'd like to utilize

For the timer, then turn the Digital Crown to select the timer. When you're done, press the Digital Crown. You can add a timer to these faces: Chronograph, Color, Mickey Mouse, Modular, Simple, and Utility.

To time events with much accuracy and simplicity. The Apple smartwatch can time full events up to 10 hours, 50 minutes and maintain track of lap or split times, then show the results as a list, a graph, or live on your watch face.

The Chronograph of your watch face has the stopwatch built-in, and you can add a stopwatch to these faces: Color, Mickey Mouse, Modular, Simple, and Utility.

Switch to the stopwatch

Open the Stopwatch app, or tap the stopwatch on your watch face if you've added it or you're using the Chronograph watch face.

Tap the Start button. Tap the Lap button to record a lap or split. Tap the Stop button to record the final time. Timing continues, whereas you switch back to the watch face or open other apps. When you end, tap the Reset button or the Lap button to reset.

You can modify the composition of the timing display before, after, or during timing. Press the display tightly, despite the fact that the stopwatch is showing, and then tap Analog, Digital, Graph, or Hybrid, etc. Switch in-between analog, one-dial, and three-dial with splits.

To swipe up on the one dial analog stopwatch appeared to see a separate minute, second, and fourth dials above a scrolling list of lap times.

How to review the results

Review results on display you used for timing, or modify screens to evaluate your lap times and faster or slowest laps marked with green and red in the format you choose. If the display has a list of lap times, turn the Digital Crown to scroll.

Monitor timing from your watch face.

To keep an eye on a timing session while displaying your usual watch face, add a stopwatch to the face. Your current onwards time will be observed on the face, and you can tap it to switch to the Stopwatch app and verify your lap times.

How to stop using the stopwatch

If you're using your Stopwatch app, press the Digital Crown. If you're using the Chronograph watch face, the stopwatch controls are always on the face-tap the Lap button to reset i

CHAPTER 11

How to read and reply to messages

*I*f you want to read incoming text messages on your Apple smart Watch. You can as well reply from Apple Watch, by dictating or selecting a quick response or switch to iPhone to type a new answer.

To read a message. You'll think a notification tap or hear an alert sound when a message comes, raise Apple smart Watch to read it. Turn the Digital Crown to scroll on the Watch. Then open a discussion in the Messages app. Tap the Message symbol in the notification.

See a photo in your message

Tap the photo to view it, double-tap it to fill up the screen, and drag it to a pan. Whilst you're finished, swipe left from the edging of the photo screen to return to the chat. If you like to save the photo, open the message in the Messages app for the iPhone, and keep it.

Listen to an audio clip in your message

Tap the clip you want to listen. The clip is always deleted after two minutes to save space. If you like to keep it, tap Keep below the clip. The audio will stay for thirty days, and you can set it to remain longer than that on the iPhone: go to Settings > Messages, scroll to Audio Messages, tap Expire, then touch a value you want.

View a video with a message

In the Messages app in your Watch, tap a video in a message to begin playing the video full-screen. Tap once to display the playback controls. Double-tap to zoom out and turn the Digital Crown to regulate the volume. Then Swipe or alternatively tap the back button to return to your conversation.

Skip to the top of a long message. In Messages, tap the top of the display.

How to answer a message. If the message just came, tap its notification, turn the Digital Crown to scroll down to the bottom of the message, and then tap Reply. If it arrived a few seconds ago, swipe down on the watch face to see the message notification, tap it, then scrolls down to the bottom and tap the Reply button.

If you want to mark the message, you already read, tap Dismiss, or swipe the message. Press the Digital Crown of your Watch to dismiss the notification with no marking of the message as read.

To decide how to be notified

When open the Apple smart Watch app on iPhone, tap My Watch, then tap Messages. Tap Custom to set options for how you like it to notify you when you receive any message.

How to send and manage messages

If you want to send a new message. Open the Messages, tightly press the list of chats, then tap the New Message symbol. Tap a contact in the list of recent chat that displays, tap + in the lower left to select from your full list of contacts, or tap the Microphone button to search for somebody in your contacts or to read out a phone number.

There are many ways to write your message:

1. Use preset replies

2. Dictate new text

3. Record an audio clip

4. Send an animated image

5. If you have your iPhone on you can send a map with your location

6. You may switch to the iPhone and utilize the full keyboard to type a message

How to send a preset reply

If you want to reply to a message, you see a list of handy phrases that you can use, tap the one you wish to send it. The phrases include related responses based on the last message received and six default phrases that you can modify. To reserve your own sentences, open the Apple smart Watch app on iPhone, tap

My Watch, go to Messages> Default Replies, then tap a default reply to modify it.

If the predetermined replies are not in the language you like to use, you can modify them by switching the keyboard for that particular language in the same chat in Messages on iPhone.

If you want to cancel your first reply on Apple smart Watch, then replay over again to see the replies in the new language. If you don't like to modify keyboards, you can dictate and send an audio clip in the style of your preference.

To dictate text. Despite the fact that of creating a message or reply, tap the Microphone button, say what you want to say, then tap Done. (Please don't forget that you can speak punctuation mark, as well or instance, "did it arrive question mark"). You can also select to send the message as a text message or an audio clip, now tap your choice. If you choose an audio clip, the receiver gets a voice message to listen to, but not a text message read.

If you are using more than one language and your dictation isn't transcribed in the right language for a chat, you can still send it as an audio clip. To modify the dictation language, change the Siri language on your iPhone in Settings > General > Siri, and then start a new chat.

If you want to send dictated text as an audio clip

If you're going to send all your prescribed text as an audio clip, you don't require selecting it each time. Open the Apple smart Watch app on your iPhone, tap My Watch, go to Messages > Audio Messages, and then tap an option.

Include an animated image

Whilst creating a message or respond, tap the image button, and then swipe to look through the available images. Turn the Digital Crown to scroll down and adjust the image, for instance, turns the smile into a frowning gesture. On faces, drag left or right across the eyes or mouth to modify the expression more. To see other image types, swipe to the next pages. The last page lists traditional emoji. When you find the right icon, tap it to add it to your message, and then send it.

To share your location

If you want to send a map showing your current sites to your friend, tightly press the display while viewing the chart, and then taps Send my Location.

You should ensure that your paired iPhone, Share My Location is turned on in Settings > iCloud > Share My Location.

Do you want to see if your messages were sent? Swipe left on the conversation in the Messages conversation list.

How to view messages detail information

Tightly press the display while viewing the conversation, then taps Details. It will show the contact information of the other participant(s) in the conversation. Alternatively, swipes left on the conversation, and then tap Details.

How to delete a conversation

Swipe left on the conversation, tap Trash, and then tap the Trash to confirm.

CHAPTER 12

Digital Touch of your Apple Watch

The main function of Digital Touch is that you can send sketches, taps, or your heartbeat to your friend with an Apple SmartWatch.

To open a Digital Touch

Press the side button of your Apple Watch to see your friends, then tap a friend and tap the Digital Touch button below his photo. You only see the Digital Touch symbol if your friend has an Apple smart Watch.

To send any of a sketch, a pattern of taps, or even your heartbeat. In the screenshot that follows, the image on the left shows what is sent, and the image on the right shows the notification that has been received.

To experience a Digital Touch someone has sent, tap on a notification. Send a sketch. Draw on the screen.

Send a tap

Tap the screen to send a single tap or repeatedly tap to send a tap pattern.

Replay the tap pattern

Share your heartbeat. Place two fingers on the display until you feel your pulse and see it animated on the screen.

The E-mail on your Apple Watch

How to read mail

On your Apple smart Watch, open the Mail app, turn the Digital Crown to scroll down the message list, and then tap a message. To read the message or reply on your iPhone, swipe up on the Mail symbol in the lower-left corner of the iPhone Lock screen.

Read mail in a notification.

If you want to set Apple smart Watch to show email notifications, you can read a new message right in the notification. Tap the notification when it first displays or swipe down on the watch face to see notifications you've received, then taps an email notification.

To dismiss the notification, swipe down from the top or tap Dismiss at the end of the message.

If you don't receive notifications for an email, go to Settings > Notifications' on your iPhone and verify to see if you have notifications turned on for e-mail.

Your Apple watch configures most text styles and some formats; quoted text displays in a different color relatively than as an indentation. If you receive an HTML message with compound elements, Apple smart Watch tries to display a text alternative of the message. It is better to try reading the message on your iPhone in its place. Switch to iPhone. Some messages are simpler to understand in full-on iPhone, wake your iPhone, and then swipe up on the email symbol in the lower-left corner of the lock screen.

Then go back to the top of a long email message. Turn the Digital Crown to scroll down swiftly, or tap the top of the display.

How to open Phone or Maps

Tap a phone number in a mail message to open Phone, or an address to open Maps.

Observe the complete address or subject line. Tap the field or the subject line. Apple watch opens the mail message in its own window; as a result, you can see all the details.

To reply to an email. You require using iPhone to create a reply-just wake your iPhone and swipe up on the mail symbol in the lower-left corner of the Lock screen.

How to manage your email

Flag a mail message. When you're reading the message in Mail on Apple smart Watch, tightly press the display, and then tap Flag. If you're looking at the message list, swipe left on the message, then tap More. You can fag the message if you preview it in a notification. You should swipe to the Flag button at the bottom of the message. You can also unplug a message that has previously been flagged.

Whenever you swipe left on a message thread, the action you select are such Flag, Mark as Unread, or Delete to the thread.

To modify the style flag. Open the Apple smart Watch app on your iPhone, tap My Watch, and then go to Mail > Custom > Flag Style.

Mark an email as read or unread.

When you're reading a message in Mail on Apple smart Watch, tightly press the display, and then taps Unread or Read. If you're looking at the message list, swipe left on the message, and then taps More.

To delete your email

If you're reading the message in Mail on Apple smart Watch, tightly press the display, then tap Trash. If you're looking at the message list, swipe left on the message, and then tap Trash.

You can alternatively delete a message from its notification. Scroll down to the bottom of the message, and then tap Trash.

However, if your account is placed to archive messages, you'll see an Archive button as an alternative of a Trash button.

How to select which mailbox appears on Apple smart Watch. Open your Apple Watch app on iPhone, tap My Watch, then go to Mail > Include Mail. You can indicate only one mailbox, although if you don't select a mailbox, you can see all the content from all inboxes.

To customize alerts

To adapt your alert open the Apple smart Watch app on iPhone, tap My Watch, then turn on Mail > Show Alerts. Tap every account or group, turn on the option to be alerted, and then select Sound or Haptic.

To build your mail list more condensed, you may reduce the number of lines of preview text shown for every email in the list. Open the Apple smart Watch app on iPhone, tap My Watch, go to Mail > Message Preview, then select to show two lines of the message, one line, or none at all.

Phone Calls on Apple Watch

How to answer phone calls

It is a very significant idea about avoiding any distractions that might lead to dangerous situations.

Answer a call.

When you see the incoming call notification, raise your wrist to wake Apple Mart Watch and identify who's calling. Tap the Answer button on Apple Watch to chat using the microphone and speaker on Apple Watch. To scroll down to answer the call using an iPhone or send a text message in its place, turn the Digital Crown to scroll down, and then select an option.

Hold a call.

Tap on "Answer on iPhone" to put the call on hold until you can continue it on your paired iPhone. The caller hears a continual sound unless you pick up the call. If you can't find your iPhone in range, tap the ping iPhone button on Apple Watch to locate it.

Switch a call from Apple Watch to your iPhone

Whilst chatting on Apple smart Watch, swipe up on the Phone symbol in the bottom-left corner of the iPhone Lock screen. Alternatively, if your iPhone is unlocked, tap the green bar at the top of the screen.

Change the call volume.

To adjust the speaker volume when chatting on Apple Watch, turn the Digital Crown while on the call or tap the volume symbols on the screen. Tap the Mute button to mute your end of the call for an instant if you're on a conference call.

You can swiftly mute an incoming call by pressing the palm of your hand on the watch display and holding it there for 3 seconds. You must initially turn on the option in the Apple smart Watch app on iPhone. Go to My Watch > Sounds and Haptics and turn on Cover to Mute.

To send a call to voicemail

Tap on the red Decline button in the incoming call notification.

If you want to listen to voicemail, if a caller leaves a voicemail, you get a notification. Tap the Play button in the notification to listen. Nevertheless, if you like to listen to voicemail later, then open the Phone app, and tap Voicemail.

How to make phone calls

"Call Max."

If the one you're calling is one of your favorites, press the side button, turn the Digital Crown or tap their initial name, then tap the call button. If they're not in your contacts list, open the Phone app, and then tap favorites or contacts. Turn the Digital Crown to scroll down and tap the name you want to call.

The call information on Apple watch

When you're talking about the iPhone, you can view call information on your Apple

Watch in the Phone app. You can as well end the call from Apple Watch, especially if you're using earphones or a headset.

CHAPTER 13

Apple Watch Calendars and Reminders

How to verify and update your calendar

The Calendar app on Apple smart Watch shows every event you've scheduled or been invited from today to the next week. Apple Smart Watch displays events for all calendars you have used on your iPhone.

View a monthly calendar

If you like to view your calendar

Open Calendar from the Watch Home screen, or swipe up on the watch face, swipe to the Calendar glance, then tap. You can tap today's date on your watch face if you've already added the calendar to the face.

"What's your next event?"

Review today's events.

Just open the Calendar, then turn the Digital Crown to scroll. Swipe right on today's timeline or jump to the current time. To see event details, such as time, location, invite status, and notes, tap the event.

But if you like to switch among the daily timeline and a single list of your events. Tightly press the display while you're viewing a daily calendar, and then tap List or Day.

View a different day.

In Day view, swipe left on today's calendar to see the next day.

Swipe right to go back

You may not be able to see any day before today, or more than seven days total. To jump back to the current day and time, tightly press the display, then tap today. In List view, then turn the Digital Crown.

To view a full month calendar. Tap < in the upper left of any daily calendar. Tap the monthly calendar to return to Day view.

Add and change your event.

Switch to the Calendar app on your iPhone, then add the event there. If you're viewing at your calendar on Apple smart Watch, wake iPhone and swipe up on the calendar symbol in the lower-left corner of the Lock screen to open the Calendar.

"Build a calendar event titled Gym for May 20, 4 PM."

To display the date or an upcoming event on your watch face. You can add some mixture of day and date to several of the watch faces: for instant, Modular, Color, Utility, Simple, or Chronograph. The Modular, Chronograph, and Mickey Mouse faces can display the next upcoming event. Tightly press the display while looking the watch face, swipe to a face, and then tap Customize.

Respond to an invitation

If you see the invitation when it comes, swipe or turn the Digital Crown to scroll to the bottom of the notification, then tap Accept, Maybe, or Decline. If you find out the notification later, tap it in your list of notifications, then scroll and respond. If you're already in the Calendar app, now tap the event to respond.

Contact an event organizer.

If you like to email the event organizer, tightly press this display while you're viewing at the event details. To send a voice message or call, tap on the organizer's name in the event details.

Time to leave

You can to-do list a "leave now" alert based on the anticipated travel time to an event you create. Open the Calendar app on your iPhone, tap the event, tap Edit, tap Travel Time, and turn it on. You'll obtain an alert that takes travel time into account.

The settings change.

Open the Apple smart Watch app on your iPhone, tap My Watch, and then tap Calendar.

How to set and respond to reminders

When there is no reminders app on Apple smart Watch, but Apple Watch notifies you of reminders you make in the Reminders app on your iPhone. And on any other or Mac, that's signed in using your Apple ID. You can make reminders using Siri on Apple smart Watch.

Respond to a reminder.

If you see the reminder notification when it comes, swipe to the bottom of the reminder, and then tap Snooze, Completed, or Dismiss. If you find out the notification afterward, tap it in your list of notifications, then scroll down and respond.

Set a reminder.

To utilize Siri on Apple Watch

Press and hold the Digital Crown, then speak. Alternatively, raise your wrist and say, "Hi Siri, set a reminder." You can set reminders on your iPhone or another device such as an IOS device or Mac that is signed in using your Apple ID.

CHAPTER 14

Your health and fitness

How to track your daily activity

The Activity app on your Apple Watch keeps a trail of your association all over the day and helps suppose you to meet your fitness set goals. The app can also track how frequently you stand up, how greatly you move, and how many minutes of exercise you perform, and it provides an easy graphic ring of your daily activity. The main goal is to sit less, move more, and get some exercise by finishing each ring every day. The Activity app on your iPhone keeps a long-term record of all your daily and weekly activity.

However, you should take note that Apple Watch can detect the heart rate using its sensor, and the Apple SmartWatch apps are not medical devices and intended solely for fitness purposes only.

Getting started

For the first time, you open Activity on your Apple smart Watch, swipe left to read the Move, Exercise, and Stand descriptions, then tap Get Started. Enter the essential information by tapping Sex, Age, Weight, and Height, and then turn the Digital Crown to set and tap Continue. Lastly, tap Start Moving.

You should also enter your birthdates, sex, height, and weight in the Apple smart Watch app on iPhone. In the Apple Watch app, tap My Watch, and then tap Health.

Verify your progress.

Swipe up on your watch face, then swipe to the Activity glance at every time to see how you're doing. Tap the glance to open the Activity app and swipe to see the personal activities. The Move ring indicates how many active calories you've burned. The Exercise ring shows how many minutes of brisk activity you've done. The Stand ring shows how many times in the day you've stood for at least 1 minute per hour. Swipe up on an activity or turn the Digital Crown to see your progress as a form of a graph.

An overlapping ring means you've exceeded your goal. Watch for achievement awards, if you have that feature turned on.

Check your activity history

To open the Activity app on your iPhone, tap on a date in the calendar to see a breakdown for that day. You'll see how many steps you took and the particular distance you covered, in addition to Move, exercise, and Stand info.

Regulate your goals.

Open Activity on Apple smart Watch and tightly press the display until you see the prompt to modify your Move goal.

On Monday, every week, you'll also be notified about the previous week's achievements, and you can regulate your daily Move goal for the coming week. Apple Watch suggests goals based on your prior performance.

Control activity notifications.

Reminders can help you when it comes to meeting goals. Apple Smart Watch can let you know if you're on the trail or falling behind your activity goals. It can even alert you if you've been sitting for too long. To select which reminders and alerts you'd like to see, open the Apple smart Watch app on your iPhone, tap My Watch, then tap Activity.

Monitor your workouts

The Workout app on your Apple Watch gives you the tools to control your personal workout sessions. It lets you set explicit goals, likes time, distance, or calories, then trails your progress, nudges you along the way, and précised your results. You can also use the Activity app on your iPhone to analysis your entire workout history.

Start a workout.

Open Workout, and then tap the workout kind you're going. As you use the app and select workouts, the order of workouts will reflect your preferences.

On your goal screen, swipe left and right to select a calorie, time, or distance goal (or no goal), then turn the Digital Crown or tap + / - to set. When you're prepared to go, tap Start. If you measure caloric or time, you can leave your iPhone at the back and exercise with just Apple smart Watch. However, for the perfect distance measurements outdoors, it better to take iPhone along.

The Outdoors and Indoor Walk, Run, Cycle differ workouts because the Apple smart Watch calculates the calorie burn another way for each. For example, the indoor workouts, Apple Watch relies mostly on your heart rate readings for calorie estimates, but for outdoor workouts, Apple smart Watch works in combination with your iPhone that has GPS to calculate speed and distance. Those standards, values, along with your heart rate, it is used to estimate the number of calories burned.

Checking your progress

To check the completion ring throughout your workout for a swift sign of your progress. Swipe on the lower half of the screen to review elapsed time, average pace, distance covered, calories used, and heart rate. As an alternative to viewing the progress rings, you can select to see your distance, calorie, or time values numerically. Open the Apple smart Watch app on iPhone, tap My Watch, then turn on Workout > Show Goal Metric.

Pause and resume.

If you want to pause the workout at any given time, tightly press the display, and then tap Pause. In the way to carry on, tightly press the display again, then tap Resume.

Conserve power at long workout

You can save power by disabling the heart rate sensor during long walking and running workouts. Your calorie burn estimate might not be as correct. Open the Apple smart Watch app on iPhone, tap My Watch, and then turn on Workout > Power Saving Mode.

End the workout.

Whenever you reach your state goal, you'll hear an alarm. If you're feeling fine and want to continue, go ahead. Apple smart Watch continues to collect data until you notify it to stop.

When you're ready, tightly press the display, and then tap end. Turn the Digital Crown to scroll through the results summary, then tap Save or Discard at the bottom.

Review your workout account.

Just open the Activity app on your iPhone, then tap a date. Scroll down to see your workouts listed there the Move, Stand, and Exercise summaries. Swipe left on a workout to see more details of it.

How to check your heart rate

If you want to get the best results, the back of the Apple smartwatch needs skin contact for the appearance like wrist detection, haptic notifications, and the heart rate sensor. Wearing an Apple smart Watch with the right fit. You must not wear it too tight, but also not too loose, and with room for your skin to breathe, this will keep you comfortable and allow the sensors to do their function.

You may yearn for tightening Apple smart Watch for workouts, and then loosen the band when you're done. Furthermore, the sensors will solely work only when you wear Apple smart Watch on the top of your wrist.

View your present heart rate.

Swipe up on the watch face, then swipe to the Heartbeat glance to determine your heart rate and see your last reading. Just tap the heart in the glance to take a new reading.

Heart rate checking during a workout

Swipe on the lower half of the workout progress screen.

How to keep your Apple Watch data accurate

Apple Watch always uses the bio-data information you give about your height, weight, gender, and age to compute how many calories you burn, how distance you travel, and other data. In addition, the more you run with the workout app you have, the more

Apple smartwatch learns your fitness rank. Moreover, the more precisely it can calculate approximately the calories you've burned during aerobic activity.

Your iPhone GPS, permit Apple smart Watch to achieve even more for accuracy. For instance, if you carry an iPhone while using the Workout app on the run, Apple smart Watch uses the iPhone GPS to calibrate your stride out. Then later, if you're not carrying the iPhone, or if you're working out where a GPS network is not available (for instance, if you are indoors), Apple smartwatch uses the already stored information about your stride to measure distance.

Update on your height and weight.

Just open the Apple smart Watch app on iPhone, tap My Watch, tap Health, Weight, or Height, and change.

CHAPTER 15

Apple Watch Pay and Passbook

How to make a purchase with Apple Pay

*I*f you want to purchase things online, you can use Apple Pay on Apple smart Watch to make purchases in stores that acknowledge contactless payments. Set up an Apple Pay in the Apple smart Watch app on your iPhone, and now you can make purchases, even if you don't have an iPhone.

If you unpaired Apple Watch, disable your passcode, or turn of wrist detection because you can't use Apple Pay.

You can add up to 8 credit or debit cards; they'll appear at the top of the stack in your Passbook app, above your passes. The last 4 or 5 digits of your credit or debit card number is shown on the front of a payment card.

Get set up on Apple Pay on your Apple Watch.

Despite the fact that you've already set up an Apple Pay on your iPhone using the Passbook app, you also need to add the credit or debit cards to use on Apple smart Watch. Have your credit or debit card handy, and then open the Apple smart Watch app on your iPhone. Tap My Watch, tap Passbook, and Apple Pay, tap Add Credit or Debit

Card, and then tap Next. If you get a supported credit or debit card on file with iTunes or the App Store, enter the card's security code first. Or else, use the iPhone camera to snap the information on your credit or debit card, and then compete in any information required, with the card security code. You must know that your card issuer sometimes requires other detail steps to prove your identity. If so, select a verification option, tap Verify, and then tap Enter Code to complete your verification.

Add another credit or debit card.

In your Apple watch app on iPhone, tap My Watch, tap Passbook & Apple Pay, tap Add Credit or Debit Card, then follow the on-screen commands.

Select your default card.

In your Apple watch app on your iPhone, tap My Watch, tap Passbook & Apple Pay, tap

Default Card, and then choose the desired card.

How to make payment for a purchase

If you want to pay for any purchase. Just double click the side button, swipe to modify cards, and then hold Apple smart Watch within a few centimeters of the contactless card reader, with the display facing the reader. A gentle pulse and tone authenticate the payment information was sent.

Find the device account number for a card.

Whenever you make a payment with Apple Watch, the Device Account Number of the card is sent with the payment to the merchant party. To find the last 4 or 5 digits of this number, open the Apple smart Watch app on iPhone, tap My Watch, tap Passbook & Apple Pay, then tap a card.

Remove a card from Apple Pay

Just open Passbook on Apple Watch, tap to choose a card, tightly press the card, then tap delete. Alternatively, open the Apple smart Watch app on your iPhone, tap My Watch, tap Passbook & Apple Pay, tap the card, then tap Remove.

If the Apple smartwatch is stolen or lost

Whenever your Apple Watch is lost or stolen, sign in to your account at iCloud.com and remove your cards. Go to Settings > My Devices, select the device, and click Remove All. You can also call the company on your cards.

How to use Passbook

Your Passbook app on Apple Watch can keep your boarding passes, movie tickets, loyalty cards, and much more in one place. Your passes in Passbook on your iPhone automatically sync to Apple Watch when you've turned on Mirror iPhone in the Watch app. Firstly scans a pass on Apple smart Watch to verify in for a fight, get into a movie, or redeem a coupon. To set options for your passes on Apple smart Watch, open the Apple Watch app on your iPhone, tap My Watch, then tap Passbook & Apple Pay.

Ways to use a pass.

If a notification for a pass shows on Apple smart Watch, tap the notification to display the pass. You may have to scroll down to get to the barcode. Alternatively, open Passbook, choose the pass and then present the barcode on the pass to the scanner.

The way to rearrange passes

On your iPhone, open the Passbook app, and drag to rearrange passes. The order will reflect on the Apple smartwatch.

When done with a pass? To delete the pass on your iPhone, Just open the Passbook app, tap the pass, tap, and then tap Delete.

CHAPTER 16

Apple Watch Maps and Directions

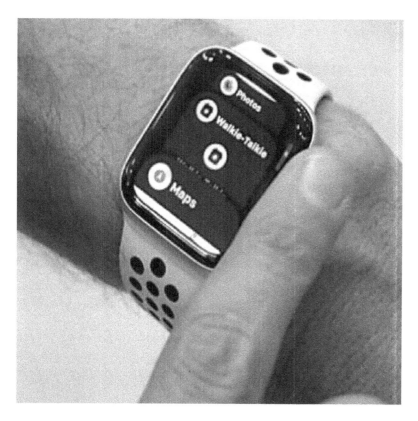

How to explore the map

Your Apple smart Watch has a Maps glance for a swift look at your surrounding location, and a full Maps app for exploring and getting directions.

"Show town on the map."

View a map.

Just open the Maps app on the Apple smartwatch. Or, for a fast look at your location, swipe up on your watch face, then swipe to the Maps glance. Tap the Maps glance to open the full Maps app.

Pan and zoom.

If you want to pan the map, drag with one finger. But if you want to zoom in or out, turn the Digital Crown. You can double-tap the map to zoom in on the spot you tap. Tap the tracking button in the lower-left to get back to your recent location.

Searching the map

As you are viewing the map, tightly press the display, tap Search, and then tap Dictate or tap a location in the list of places you've explored recently.

Getting data about the landmark or location

Just tap the location on the map, then turn the Digital Crown to scroll the information. Tap < in the upper left to return to the map.

To stick a pin

Just touch and hold the map where you want the pin to go, wait for the pin to drop, and then let go. At the moment you can tap the pin for address information, or utilize it as the starting point or destination for directions. To move the pin, drop a new one in the new location.

How to find any location on the world map

Here drop a pin on the location, then tap the pin to see address information.

To call a location

Just tap the phone number in the location information. To switch to iPhone, swipe up on the Phone symbol in the lower-left corner of the Lock screen, then tap the green bar at the top of the screen.

How to see your contact's address on the map

As you are viewing the map, tightly press the display, tap Contacts, turn the Digital Crown to scroll, and then tap the contact.

Get your location.

Just open Maps, then tap the recent location arrow in the lower left. Or swipe to the Maps glance, which always indicates where you are. If you have a future calendar event, the Maps glance shows directions to it.

How to get your directions

If you want to get your directions to any landmark or map pin. Just open Maps, then tap the target landmark or map pin. Scroll down the location detail until you see Directions, then tap Walking or Driving. Whenever you're all set to go, tap Start, then follow the directions.

To get directions to a search result or contact. As you are viewing the map, tightly press the display, and then tap Search or Contacts.

To ask Siri for directions

Just say to Siri where you'd like to go.

How to follow the directions

Subsequent to your tap to start and head off on your first leg, Apple smart Watch uses tapping to allow you to know when to turn. A stable series of 12 taps means turn right at the intersection you're approaching; three pairs of two taps means turn left. But if not sure, what your target location look like? You'll feel a vibration when you're on the last leg, and again when you arrive.

Just swipe left on the current step of your directions, or tap the dots at the bottom of the screen to see a map view.

How to estimated time

Just of arrival, tightly press to stop directions. To find out when you'll get there.

Just look in the upper-left corner for your estimated time of arrival. The current time is in the upper right.

The end directions prior to you get there

Tightly press the display, and then tap Stop Directions.

Play music on your iPhone

You can use the Music app or the Now Playing glance on Apple Watch to control music playback on your iPhone.

"Play Panda Bear."

Play music on the iPhone.

Just open Music to Apple smart Watch. Surf through playlists, albums, artists, or songs until you see a list of songs you like, and then tap a song to play it.

But if you don't spot the music you're expecting, make sure iPhone, not Apple Watch, is your source. Tightly press the display, tap Source, then Return to the tracklist.

Tap to see the album art. Firmly press for playback options. Skip to previous or next track. Tap -/+ or turn Digital Crown to adjust the volume.

See album art for the existing song. Tap the album name above the playback controls. Tap again to return to the controls.

To send audio to another device with AirPlay. As you are viewing the playback controls, tightly press the display, tap AirPlay, then select a destination.

To shuffle or repeat songs

As you are viewing the playback controls, tightly press the display, then tap Shuffle or Repeat.

Controlling playback with the glance

Just use the Now Playing glance for swift control. Swipe up on the watch face, then swipe to the playback controls. But if you don't see the Now Playing glance, open the Apple Watch app on your iPhone, tap My Watch, then turn on Music > Show in Glances.

How to play music on Apple watch

You can store your music on Apple smart Watch and then listen to it via Bluetooth headphones or speakers without your iPhone close.

Store a song on Apple Watch.

Just open the Apple Watch app on your iPhone, tap My Watch, go to Music>Synced Playlist, then select the playlist of songs you like to move to Apple smart Watch.

Then, put the Apple smartwatch on its charger to entire the sync.

While the music has been synced, open the Settings app on Apple Watch, go to General > about, and look below Songs to see the number of songs copied.

You can also use the Music app on the iPhone to make a playlist specifically for music you want to listen to on Apple smart Watch.

How to pair Bluetooth headphones or speakers

You should follow the instruction guide that came with the headphones or speakers to set them in discovery mode.

When the Bluetooth device is ready, open the Settings app on Apple smart Watch, tap Bluetooth, then tap the device when it displays.

To play songs stored on Apple smart Watch.

Just open Music on Apple Watch, tightly press the display, tap Source, then select Watch.

To control playback

Swipe to the Now Playing glance for swift control. Swipe up on the watch face, then swipe to the playback controls. You can control playback using the Music app.

How to limit the songs stored

Just open the Apple Watch app on your iPhone, tap My Watch, go to Music> Playlist Limit, then select a storage limit or the maximum number of songs to be stored on Apple smart Watch.

See how music is stored on the Apple smartwatch.

Just on Apple smart Watch, open the Settings app, go to General > about, and look under Songs.

CHAPTER 17

Using an Apple smart Watch as Remote Control

How to control music on your PC

Y*ou can use the Remote Application on the Apple smartwatch to play music in iTunes on your computer on the same Wi-Fi network.*

Add an iTunes library.

Just open the remote App on Apple smart Watch, then tap Add Device +. In iTunes on your PC, click the Remote button close to the top of the iTunes window, and then enter the 4-digit code displayed on Apple smart Watch.

Don't stare for the Remote button in iTunes before you tap Add Device on Apple Watch-the button shows only when a remote is trying to connect. In iTunes twelve and later, the Remote button is in the upper left, under the Volume slider. But in iTunes 11 and earlier, the Remote button is in the upper right, below the Search field.

Select a library to play. If you have one library, you should be good to go. But if you're adding more than one library, tap the one you like when you open Remote on Apple smart Watch.

If you're already playing music, tap the back button in the upper left of the playback controls, and then tap the library.

To control playback. Just use the playback controls in the Remote App.

The way to remove a library

In your Remote App on Apple Watch, tap the Back button in the upper left to view your devices, tightly press the display, then tap Edit. When the device symbol jiggle, tap x on the one you like to remove, then tap Remove. If that was your only remote device, you're finished. Or else, tap the checkmark to finish editing.

How to control Apple TV with Apple Smart Watch

You can also use Apple smart Watch as a remote control for your Apple TV when you're connected to the same Wi-Fi network.

Pairing Apple smartwatch with your Apple TV

If the iPhone has never joined the Wi-Fi network that Apple TV is on, join it now. Then, open the Remote App on Apple Watch and tap Add Device +. On your Apple TV, go to Settings > General >

Remotes, select your Apple watch, and then enter the passcode displayed on Apple smart Watch.

When the pairing successfully, an icon appears next to Apple Smart Watch, it's ready to control your Apple TV.

How to control Apple TV

You must make sure that your Apple TV is awake. Open the Remote App on Apple smart Watch, select Apple TV, and then swipe up, down, left, or right to move through Apple TV menu options.

Tap to select the selected item. Tap the Menu button to go back, or touch and hold it so that to return to the top menu. Tap the Play/Pause button to pause or resume to playback. Tap to go back or touch and hold to return to the main menu.

Control another device.

Swipe to move through Apple TV menu options;

Tap to select.

Play or pause selection.

To Unpaired and remove Apple TV.

Just on your Apple TV, go to Settings > General> Remotes, then choose your Apple smart Watch under iOS Remotes to remove it. Then, open the Remote App on Apple smart Watch and, when the "lost link" message appears, tap Remove.

CHAPTER 18

Things you need to know about a new Apple Watch.

The Apple Watch has been released recently, it comes with many things you didn't know. So we are going to tell you about the tips that you didn't know about Apple Watch Series 5. The recent design of Apple Watch was better than the previous models. Firstly, what to do when you get a new Apple Watch, the first thing you need to do is the ability to make use of a great new inforgraph of your Watch, that will take you to the entire Apple Watch face. Of course, this is greater than the previous generation of Apple Watch.

Here there are many different functions, from the walkie talkie, weather and many more. However, you might scroll down to anyone you want, ranging from a one that more center for you.

From timer, an activity, you can also change these around moving your Location to where you like in the Watch. When that's done, the next thing to do is to center areas of your Watch. You may choose a different setting such as the digital crown, time, the earth, and even measuring your heart rate as well as setting the inner configurations such as time. Here you may even choose a different clock face pattern and different like wake-up application.

In the inforgraph, you can set different clock faces. This new inforgraph is unique concerning the Apple Watch series.

The next thing to do is set the inforgraph-up you want to mark it. With this, you can open your Mac book, but only when you log in into your Watch. We want to do the basic setting, go to security, and allow your Apple Watch to make your Mac that is simple and can be easily paired with your Mac, Mac-pro, or any type of Mac do have to use your Apple Watch.

The next thing you may want to do is to set Activity shearing. Open up the activity on your phone, then go to the sharing button, you can see that you can invite your friends. From your Watch App on your phone, you can increase the brightness of your Watch. Besides, you can as well change the textures to increase the size of the text where it is a little bit easier to read messages, but you may make it a little bit smaller.

The next features you are going to set up when you get a new Apple Watch is the most serious features. I hope you will not use it. Still, it is better to set up because it is very important to have it in your Apple Watch. So it is an emergency response system of your Watch. From your phone, open Apple Watch App for a phone. It allows you to call the emergency number in which you are going to include the number into the App. So if you set it up, it could reach that number in case of an emergency that number could get a notification that you need help.

Another thing that is very important is setting up a fall detection. This App will ask whether Watch has fallen or not within your hand reach; it will automatically ask you so that you have the ability to make sure you Watch is safe.

Another important setup is to set —up your heart rate so that if you are in a workout, it will appear active, you can set the haptic feature so that to send the information to your emergency contact when needed.

Another good app is using the eBay app that you should download on your phone open it in safari browser, and it is a wonderful app that I'm sure when you download it, you will enjoy it. Open the new page and write a bitly getbetes bonus

Which you can get 10% back bonus from eBay cashback. Write your email and download the eBay app. That App contains a 10% cash guaranty. It has VIP 30% and all coupons that available for purchase, and you can also download it on your computer. When you check any marketplace online, you will see the coupon code, such as Walmart, JXV, Dr. ax, and eBay. You can click on the shop now. But mark you Amazon does not have that 10% cashback guarantee. You can do all there exactly eBay when clicking the shop now. I highly recommended using this App because I usually use it to buy online and get a 10% discount.

Another thing you will do when you get a new Apple Watch series 4.On your phone can explore the whole gallery of your Watch, you may view inforgraph and select any Watch face you like. You can also view all applications for your Apple Watch, and you may get many applications for your Apple Watch for better performances.

If you want to set and optimize your Watch go to the setting on your Watch open setting, you can set it up to 15,30, and 70 minutes here, you can set how long you want your Watch to stay in standby.

How to use Apple Watch

The Apple Watch may perhaps not have become as very important as your smartphone. Since Apple first took the veil of secrecy of its smartwatch in 2015. The Apple Watch has motionlessly managed to fill a need for many users, and in addition to the cellular connectivity in the latest series makes this gadget even more valuable. The key to making the Apple Watch Series 4 an essential part of your life? So it is very important to know how to get the most of it. We have an in-depth guide to Apple's Watch, but let's begin with some quick tips and tricks that put up the Apple Watch even easier to use.

Switching between Apple Apps

If you want to switch between your Apps, to go back to your most recently used apps, double-tap the Digital Crown.

Switching in-between your Watch Face

You might need to set up multiple watch faces for different purposes - one with a minimum face for those times when you don't like a cluttered edge, the other with a more fun display. To switch back and forth, you can swipe to the left and right from the watch face.

Rearranging your applications in the Dock

Apple Watch could overhaul the Dock, which gives you simple access to your most frequently used apps. However, what if you want to change the order in which those apps appear how to about it.

Just Open the Watch application on your iPhone and select Dock.

Select whether you want your Dock ordered by recently used apps or favorites. Tap Edit to choose your favorite apps in your Watch. You can add up to Ten apps to your Dock, which is available by pressing the side button on your watch device.

Muting an Incoming Call

When a call comes in, when you are in the middle of a meeting, cover your Apple Watch with your hand to silent it.

How to Take a Screenshot

Whenever you like to take a screenshot with your Apple Watch, primarily, make sure that the feature is enabled in the Watch app on your iPhone. Then Tap General from the Watch app's main screen, scroll down, and tap Enable Screenshots.

When this feature enabled, to take a screenshot, you should press the Digital Crown and the Side Button at the same time (Alternatively, hold the Digital Crown and then press the Side Button). The Screenshots are stored in the Camera Roll on your iPhone.

To Send a Friend Your Location

It's very easy to let your friends know where you are, using the Messages app on your Apple Watch. Open a conversation in the Messages. Vigor Touch the screen and tap Send Location.

Reading and responding to messages

To read a new message in your Watch, raise your wrist after reading a message notification. But, to dismiss the message, lower your arm.

Sending a text message

If you want to send a new text, open the Apple Watch's Messages app. Its icon, a sign is identical to the one on your iPhone. Force Touch, the screen, then tap New Message.

How to delete email

Some tips on how to get rid of an email directly from your watch area.

On your Apple Watch, open the Mail app Swipe left on any email. Alternatively, tap the trash to delete the message.

How to clear Your Notifications

A lot of Notifications piling up? Here is how to dismiss them.

From your watch face, swipe down from the top of the screen to display your notification. Force touches the display, then tap Clear all.

How to set focus and exposure in the App camera

The camera on your Apple Watch allows you to use the Watch as a remote for your iPhone camera. Launch the App, and tap any place on the preview image on your Watch to set the focus and exposure.

Pausing or ending your workout

With a workout in progress, open the Workout app. Swipe right on display. Tap End or Pause.

Deleting Apps from Your Watch

If you want to delete Apps from Watch, Deleting an app from your Apple Watch works in a similar way it does on an iPhone. From the face of your Apple Watch or any app, press the Digital Crown to go to the Watch's home screen.

Tap and hold any app icon. Tap the small X that appears on any third-party app icon to remove the app from your Apple Watch. Then Tap Delete App to confirm.

Changing Audio sources

The tricks to control the device, your phone, or your Watch. From which you play music. In the Music app, Force Touch the display and then taps Source.

Choose the iPhone to play music on the phone. Select Apple Watch to play music from your Watch on a Bluetooth speaker and headphone.

How to Switch Views in a Calendar

Open the Calendar app, and then select a day, and then Force Touch the display.

Select to view a list of upcoming events or Up Next to see the cards of upcoming events. Tap

Today to skip to the current day in either view.

The Apple Watch has two different faces versions featuring either Mickey or Minnie Mouse. Also, they can pull off a little trick.

How to switch to the Mickey/Minnie Mouse watch face

Tap the screen, and any character that you have selected will announce the current time. (You can also disable this under Sounds & Haptics in either the Apple Watch's Settings app or the Watch app on your iPhone.)

How to Activate Siri

To activate Siri, pull up Siri for voice commands, Press and hold the Digital Crown on the Watch. Otherwise, raise your wrist and say, "Hey Siri."

How to Find Your Phone

Your phone is constantly a quick tap away when you're wearing an Apple Watch.

On the watch face, swipe up on display to bring up Control Center. Then tap the Find Phone icon in the right. It will make Your iPhone play a sound.

How to unpaired Your Apple Watch

If you want to upgrade your iPhone, you'll make sure you unpair it with your Apple Watch. Open the Apple Watch app on your iPhone and choose your Apple Watch from the main menu.

On the Apple Watch next screen, tap the "i" button next to your Watch.

Tap the Unpair Apple Watch. (Remember this will back up all settings from your Apple smart Watch onto your iPhone and then erase your Apple Watch.)

How to Call Emergency Services

The first Emergency SOS was added into 2016's Watch three updates. However, this can also work on Apple series 4.

If you like to call emergency service, Press and hold the Apple Watch's Side Button; the power of the menu will appear, but continue to hold the Side Button until the SOS countdown displays. (On the other hand, instead of holding the Side Button, you can slide the emergency SOS control of the power of menu.)

By the end of the Apple Watch countdown, your local emergency services will be called. (However, if you like to cancel the emergency call, release the button before the end of the countdown.

After the call, your emergency contacts that already set in the health app on your iPhone will automatically be notified, and even if the Location Services on your Watch are off, it will be temporarily activated.

CHAPTER 19

Best Apple watches Applications

*T*hese are the list of some selected applications for your Apple Watch.

Health and Fitness Apps

Sleep++

One important thing that the Apple Watch doesn't yet accomplish is helping you figure out how well you're sleeping. Because of that, David Smith, developer of Pedometer++ a health and fitness apps, takes up that niche with his Sleep++ App, this App uses the Apple Watch's built-in sensors to track your hours of sleeping and waking. For using this App, activate the App on your Apple Watch when you go to bed, again when you get up in the morning, and it'll provide you an idea of how restful your night's sleep has been.

Lose It!

The Apple Watch is attractive solid at helping you track your daily activity, but when it comes to fitness, the other end of the spectrum is tracking your food intake. That's where Lose It! Apples come in. This App can give you an insight look at your current calorie budget for the whole day, your number of steps, your intake of nutrients, and it can even know how you're doing for the week. For your good health, you can log your calories for your meals by Force pressing on the main screen - no need to pull out your phone.

Pedometer

The pedometer is one of the fitness App. Fitness has emerged as one major selling point for the Apple Watch. And as supportive as the three rings in the Watch's Activity app might be, occasionally you want hard data. Pedometer++ uses the accelerometer and sensors in both your phone and your Apple Watch to track how many steps you take every day. The App rewards you when you hit your goal with a shower of virtual confetti. It also has a built-in watch face barrier, so your step count and the distance you've walked is never more than a glance away.

Nike + Run Club

If you don't have one of those fancy Apple Watch Nike+ models, you can still get the advantage of the company's workout app through the Nike+ Run Club app. It allows you to set goals for workout distance, duration, or speed, plus supporting voice over cues; the App can auto-pause when you stop running and running on treadmills. It also has bundles of a motivational aspect; focus you the weather for the day and allowing you to schedule an upcoming run, and displaying the current playlist of your music.

News

Overcast

Sometimes you may not feel like to listen to podcasts on your Apple Watch, but the Overcast App gives you control podcast playback from your phone, with controls to play and pause or jump back or forward 30 seconds. You can toggle Overcast's effects, like Voice Boost, Smart Speed, and adjust the playback speed. This App, also shows you what's up next in your playback queue, as well as allowing you to generate new playlists on the fly.

Weather Apps

Carrot Weather

Apple Watch has a built-in Weather app, which is fine as things go, but if you like to delve into something a bit more comprehensive (and a bit more detailed), Carrot Weather may be just what the meteorologist ordered. This App will give you the current conditions, a look at what the day holds, and even a little quip to keep things interesting. You can also toggle to multiple locations, and there is a watch face complication, which includes both current conditions and temperature.

Anthy

Are you among the security-conscious people? If yes, this App is right for you. You probably have many websites that use two-factor authentication. This a great app for good and maintenance track of all those two-factor codes, and the Apple Watch app lets you reclaim them right from your wrist instead of having to dig through your phone to find them. It has also come with a little time out bar that shows you how long you have before the code refreshes again.

Just Press Record

Another wonderful app, with another entry in the "quick notes" category, is the self-described Just Press Record by Open Planet Software. The main strength of this App is in letting you record swift audio notes. But the App may not be enough for your podcast needs, but you can also record, playback, and save those audio notes, which are synced via the cloud Drive to your iPhone. It can as well add transcriptions to short notes.

PCalc

If you don't want a calculator watch at a point? TLA Systems's Pcalc is on apparently every Apple platform, so an Apple watch edition is a natural fit. This admired calculator not only offers basic math operations, but also includes a built-in tip calculator and bill splitter, input utilizing dictation or Scribble, and it comes with handy conversion and mathematical constant functions.

Navigation Apps

Citymapper

If you want to get around town, then Citymapper is an Apple Watch app for you. It handles much all forms of public transportation within the city, as well as giving options for biking, walking, and driving. There is swift access to saved destinations, as well as it is an ability to bring up nearby transit stops and spot when the next bus or train arrives.

Travelling

Yelp

When do you like to find a great nearby restaurant, coffee shop, or bar? The Yelp app here is the answer that will help you and to make it quick. You can scan through the listings of nearby businesses, and quickly glance at ratings and reviews, and pull up directions to the Location via the Apple Watch's Maps app. With Yelp App on your Apple Watch, you'll never go hungry again.

Lyft

Do you need a ride? The Lyft app can help you make that happen. It's a trouble-free and straightforward offering that lets you know how long it'll procure a car to get to your Location. One of the pleasant features it offers over some other ride-sharing apps is that it additionally lets you enter a different pickup location through voice dictation.

Sports Apps

MLB.com At Bat

When you need the best number up-to-the-minute baseball scores without conceivably looking like you're checking the scores? MLB. Com's At Bat app can assist by putting them right on your wrist. You know how to check the current scoreboard or skim via a list of teams to see how your favorites are doing on the baseball game.

Music Apps
Shazam

Shazam offers its excellent music-recognition skills to your Apple Watch very well. It is no longer that you have to fish out your phone fast enough to play "name that tune" launch the Shazam app on your Apple Watch, tap the button, and I'll listen to whatever's playing, and it even shows you a match and lyrics likely.

Productivity Apps
Fantastical 2

This is among the best productivity apps for calendaring, and there aren't many apps that will be aligned with Fantastical. Apple's built-in gift, Fantastical, offers a scrollable list of imminent appointments for the week, detailed views of events, and even your to-do items. You can also create a new event using dictation and get a glance at your upcoming events with your Apple watch face complication.

Drafts

If you like to give the impression of being captured with ideas when you're on the go? Just look no for Agile Tortoise's Drafts. It is an Apple Watch app that is ideal for those quick notes that bang into your head. When you launch the app, then tap the microphone icon to record a quick note, which will be transcribed into text and filed into your inbox. But If you like, you can make use of the Advanced Capture options to insert an emoticon or watch OS's Scribble feature to enter your text letter by letter. Also, you can even append, prepend, trash, or individual archive notes in your inbox.

Reference Apps

Microsoft Translator

We may still be a far ways from the general translator of Star Trek, but apps like Microsoft Translator can still help a lot. With the Apple Watch version of this App, you can use dictation to speak a phrase and then have it translated into one of a number of languages. You will be able to see a text version of the translation and still, in some cases, hear it spoken aloud. Moreover, you can save frequently used snippets for future reference.

Finance Apps

Square Cash

This another great App for finance if you get it on your Apple watch. That is means you don't need to reach for your wallet or your phone next time you need to send a friend some money. In its place, you can do it all from the Apple watch with the Square Cash app. Just tap on a contact from the list.

Whichever you may like, either someone you've recently sent money to or anyone in your contact list. Just select the amount of tapping the bill icons. You can tap more than once, so if you want to send $12, tap the $10, followed by the $1 twice. Then send the money over, and you're square cash it! This is great!.

CHAPTER 20

Apple watches the best games.

*A*pple Watch games provide the crucial quick fix, allowing you to solve puzzles. And hack away at enemies for a few minutes exclusive of going through the trouble of pulling out your phone. Favorites such as Trivia Crack make a perfect fit for the Apple Watch's display, while text-based adventures such as SpyCatcher control the wearable computer to make you feel like you're a character in a sci-fi movie.

Pokémon Go

When you enormously, positively, must catch them all, sticking to your iPhone won't suffice. Luckily, Pokémon Go provides an Apple Watch app that lets you carry out certain responsibilities, like incubating eggs that you've collected through physical activity. The more you walk or exercise, the closer those eggs get to hatching. You can as well visit Pokéstops, earn some candy, and be alerted to nearby Pokémon, without the need to pull out your phone.

Komrad

Komrad is a text adventure game composes of Part War Games, part Cold War drama, where you're recruited to assist and retrieve secret codes from an antiquated Soviet AI program. You'll chat with the AI, selecting your conversational responses, which will dictate the course of the game. Also, just in case you are curious about the plausibility, the *former Design Officer of IBM's Watson project created the game.*

Pocket Bandit

Have you ever dreamed of committing a high stakes jewel heist? Pocket Bandit fulfills that, offering up a game in which you break into safes for the sweet, sweet loot. The catch? Here you must crack the combination locks by turning your Apple Watch's Digital Crown, and then find out the number by the haptic feedback. Before the cops show up to take you away. Every safe you crack nets a different treasure, and the game continues to add more as time goes on. It's brainy, if not predominantly difficult, and, as a plus, requires no real law breaking.

Tiny Armies

A quick small strategy game, Tiny Armies puts you in charge of a number on it - tiny armies symbolized by blue squares with dots, trying to capture rival armies symbolized by red squares with xs. To do this, you swipe on blue armies to direct them but must be careful they'll move in a straight line unless they hit an obstacle, like an impenetrable mountain, drowning lakes, or confusing forests. The board layouts acquire harder as you go, but it is a good game that you can pick up and play when you have time for that.

Field Day

Field Day is a good game that does not take a green thumb to be successful. With this game, which sees you planting some crops and delivering orders, it requires the Apple Watch. As you go on, you'll engage more works and increase your farm not just to take in crops but animals as well. It's fascinating and cute, and a good game that gives way to scratch that itch to live your life as a typical farmer.

Rules!

The Apple Watch face display provides enough real estate for a first-class puzzle game, and Rules! is one of the best brain teasers game on the platform. The game starts cleanly, providing four numbered tiles and a basic rule, such as "tap in descending order." Nevertheless, since a new rule gets added with every turn, you'll swiftly find yourself racking your noggin, trying to follow them all if you want to wake up your brain on the way to work, playing Rules! It is as good a way as any.

Lifeline

At the same time as a puzzle and word games work fine on the Apple Watch. Lifeline is the main model of a unique play experience that's best to enjoy on your Apple watch. The composes of a text-based adventure in which you help a stranded astronaut named Taylor; Lifeline puts you in total control of the story by allowing you to decide how you respond to your new friend all through his dire journey. Lifeline is playable on the iPhone and iPad, but playing it on your Watch makes it truly feel like you're exchanging messages with an astronaut by way of a futuristic transmitter. If you end, in short order, no worries: you can currently check out many sequels, including Lifeline 2, Lifeline: Whiteout, Lifeline, and more.

Runeblade

The idea of playing a role-playing game on a tiny wristwatch may seem absurd, but Runeblade pulls it off. This dungeon crawler keeps it basic, allowing you to hack away at a secure stream of mystical creatures by just tapping your sword icon every few seconds. However, with rich, cartoon graphics; a perceptive upgrade system, and a secure stream of new bosses and environments to tackle, this miniature RPG is surprisingly alluring.

Trivia Crack

Trivia category-based quizzes have turned troves of iOS gamers into trivia addicts. The game's Apple Watch counterpart makes it even easier to get your fix. Trivia Crack is a colorful spinning category wheel, cutely animated font, and fun questions. Which touch on all from history to pop culture, Translate elegantly to the Apple Watch's small screen. You can still start a new game right from your wrist.

Letter Zap

Letter Zap is one of the best letter-matching game that sacrifices little in its conversion to the Apple Watch. It's as chaste as word games get; you're a task with untying as numerous words as likely in 30 seconds, with no special power-ups or unlockables to get in the way. Letter Zap's short-burst formula makes it an ideal for Apple's Watch, and the hunt for a high score will keep you playing for some time. There is a quick Apple-Watch-only challenge mode where you could have to form words while upholding your heartbeat under control.

CHAPTER 21

The Coolest Things that Apple Watch 5 Can Do

*T*he Apple Watch is an amazingly capable device, but it still doesn't take you long to master the basics of what it can do. But, once you've got those basics down, it's time to change gears and try your hand at some of the smart but less obvious features that you can take advantage of. This chapter will expose you to some of the most cooling tips and tricks that your Apple Watch could do.

An Apple Watch was made with the water resistance capability if you have a natural inclination not to get your electronics wet. While the first version via series 4 was water-resistant. Apple added the ability to submerge the watch up to 50 meters depth with the to its smartwatch line. And that feature remains a part of the Series 3 and 4model, making them perfect for workouts at the local pool. But, always remember to use the Water Lock feature to get rid of any extra water from the speaker opening after your workout. Water Lock kicks in automatically when you start a swimming workout, and you can unlock the screen and clear out the water. When you've done by turning the digital crown. You must keep it in mind that if you take a swim in the ocean, you should perhaps rinse off the saltwater with fresh water afterward.

Control your Apple TV and home theater.

Did you know that you can control an Apple TV with your Apple Watch? Or did you still remote slip between the couch cushions again? Do not mind that yet. Your Apple Watch can control many home devices while still leaves on your wrist. For instance, if you have an Apple TV, you can use the Apple Watch's Remote app to swipe roughly the set-top box's menus, start and pause playback, and more. You must get a Harmony Hub setup so that to run scripts from the Watch. To turn on and off your home theater devices, by using the IFTTT app on your Watch. Despite the fact that it will not let you do anything beyond that.

Talk to your car

If you've got a new automobile, your Apple Watch may give you ways to check on your car's status, and also, you can even interact with it. Cars such as Mercedes Benz, BMW Porsche, VW, allow you do a lot of things with Apple watch. like locking and unlocking your car's doors, honk the horn. Checking battery levels on electric vehicles, and even assist you in finding where you parked the car. But, If you've got an older car model or an aftermarket option from Viper, you must include an app to let you lock, unlock, and start your car remotely.

Compete against your friends in the fitness

Apple Watch can be used to measure yourself against your friends by turning on Activity Sharing. In the Activity app on iOS, go to the Sharing tab and tap the Plus (+) icon in the top right of your Watch to invite a friend to share their Activity info with you. Subsequently, you will be able to check their status in the Activity app on your Apple

Watch; you'll get notifications when they complete workouts.

Running without your iPhone

Speaking of working out, if you've got an Apple Watch, you can lastly live the dream and leave your iPhone behind when you go for a run around the city. Because both models of the Apple watch have built-in GPS that can track your workout without needing to lug that heavy phone in your hand or pocket. Plus, bring along a pair of Bluetooth headphones for the trip, and you can listen to music right off your Apple Watch as well. Moreover, Apple's Workout app, you are capable of taking advantage of this in abundance of third-party apps like Nike+ Run Club and runkeeper.

Stream music without your phone

You'll require an Apple Watch Series 3,4 or 5 with LTE connectivity to pull off this feat, but it's one that will be a welcome aspect if you enjoy a little music add-on your run. Because the Series 3 model can connect to wireless networks on its own, you can stream songs without having your iPhone close at hand. An ideal for working out. And you're not immediately limited to Apple Music and its ten Dollars-a-month streaming service. Apple, too, includes an app called Radio with the Apple Smart Watch for streaming songs.

Unlock your Mac

Did you know your Apple watch can save you some typing difficulty? If you've got a Mac made within several years, your Apple Watch can be used to unlock the screen without having to enter any of your passwords.

Allow your Apple Watch to unlock Mac. Now, when you wake that Mac from sleep and you're wearing your Apple Watch, it should take care of that wretched password business for you.

Scribble messages

There's no doubt, you know you can compose messages and emails on your Apple Watch through dictation, but did you also know that anywhere you can dictate a reply, you can also write one? A Scribble quality massages let you draw letters, numbers, and symbols on your screen and have them automatically transformed into text. It's amazingly good, and very useful when you're in a place where perhaps you don't want to look similar to Dick Tracy talking to your Watch. When you want to enter a response, then tap the Scribble key and write away!.

Order food

One of the coolest things that Apple Watch can do. Whenever get so hungry that even taking your phone out looks like a bridge too far? Providentially, you can order any food right from your Apple Watch, using a variety of apps. GrubHub lets you reorder recent favorites with just a couple taps, or you can purposely order a pizza from Domino's or burritos from Chipotle.

Exposure to liquid

Apple Watch is water-resistant but not waterproof. You may wear and use Apple Watch during exercise; exposure to sweat is acceptable, in the rain, and while washing your hands with water. If water splashes onto the watch, wipe it off with a nonabrasive, lint-free material. Do your best to minimize exposing Apple Watch to these substances like, Soap, detergent, acids or acidic foods, and any liquids other than freshwater, such as saltwater, soapy water, pool water, perfume, insect repellent, lotions, sunscreen, oil, adhesive remover, hair dye, or solvents.

Submerging Apple Watch in a liquid is not recommended. Apple Watch has a water resistance ranking of IPX7 under IEC standard 60529 while the leather bands are not water-resistant at all. Because water resistance is not a permanent, condition and an Apple smartwatch cannot assume or reseal for water resistance.

The following may affect the water-resistance of Apple Watch:

1. Dropping your Apple Watch or subjecting it to other impacts.

2. Submerging or sinking the watch in water for an extended period.

3. Bathing or Swimming with Apple Watch.

4. Exposing Apple Watch to any pressurized water or high-velocity water, such as showering, water skiing, Wakeboarding, surfing, jet skiing, etc.

5. Wearing it in the sauna or steam room.

How to clean Apple Watch

Always keep your Apple Watch clean and dry. Clean and dry Apple smart Watch, the band, and your skin following workouts or profound sweating. Dry Apple Watch face and the band meticulously if they are exposed to freshwater. Clean Apple Watch if exposed to everything that may cause stains, or other damage, such as dirt, sand, makeup, ink, soap, detergent, acid solution, or acidic foods. Or when comes in contact with liquids other than water, including those that may lead to skin irritation like sweat, saltwater, soapy water, pool water, perfume, insect repellent, lotions, sunscreen, oil. Others are adhesive remover, hair dye, or solvents, etc. Despite the regular care, the Apple Watch and band colors may vary or fade over a period.

Turn off Apple Watch.

Press and hold the side button of your Watch, then drag the Power Off slider to the right.

Then depress the band release buttons and remove the band.

Wipe Apple Watch clean with a nonabrasive, lint-free cloth. You may also lightly dampen the cloth with fresh water.

Dry Apple Watch with a lint-free, nonabrasive cloth.
Apple Watch (gold) models benefit the most if you clean them frequently. Clean with a nonabrasive, lint-free cloth to get rid of surface oil, perfumes, lotions, and other substances, particularly before storing the Apple Watch.

These things not recommended in the care of your Apple Smart Watch:

1. Do not clean Apple Watch at the same time as it's charging.

2. Do not dry Apple Watch, the bands using an external heat source like a hairdryer.

3. Do not use chemical cleaning products or compressed air when cleaning your Apple Watch.

The front of Apple Watch is made by Ion-X glass or sapphire crystal, each with a fingerprint-resistant oleophobic, which is oil-repellent coating substances. This coating material wears over time with regular usage. Cleaning products and abrasive substances will further diminish the coating, and may probably scratch the glass or the sapphire crystal.

You should never apply excessive pressure to a button or the Digital Crown on Apple Watch, or to force a charging connector into its port, for the reason that, this may cause damage that is not covered under the company warranty. Take note that if the connector and port don't join with reasonable ease, most likely, they don't match. Check for any obstruction and make sure that the connector matches the port and that you have placed the connector correctly in relation to the port.

Some specific usage patterns can be a factor in the fraying or breaking of cables. The cable attached to a charging component, like any other metal cable, is subject to becoming brittle or weak if repetitively bent in the same spot. This will be prevented by gentle curves instead of angles in the cable. Regularly, inspect the cable and connector for any kinks, breaks, bends, or any damage. In case you find any such loss, discontinue the use of the cable.

It is normal after regular use the lightning connector to USB cable can get discoloration. Extreme dirt, debris, and exposure to moisture may cause discoloration. If your lightning cable or connector becomes so warm during use or if Apple Watch won't charge, disconnect the cable from the power adapter and clean the lightning connector with a non-corrosive, dry, lint-free cloth. You should not use liquids or cleaning agents when cleaning the Lightning connector.

Magnetic charging cable and magnetic charging case

The Apple Watch magnetic charging cable and magnetic charging case discoloration of the charging surface may occur after regular use due to dirt and debris that come in contact with the magnetic cover. This is common. Cleaning the magnetic charging surface may reduce, or prevent, that discoloration, and will help to avoid damage to your charger and Apple smart Watch. If you want to clean the charging surface, disconnect the charger from both Apple Watch and the power adapter outlets and wipe with a damp, nonabrasive lint-free cloth.

Always dry it with a nonabrasive, lint-free cloth before charging again. it also not requires using a cleaning chemical agents when cleaning the charging surface.

Apple Watch optimum ambient temperature

Apple Watch operating temperature is designed to work best in ambient temperatures between 0° and 35°C and be stored in temperatures between -20° and 45° C. Apple Watch can be spoiled and battery life reduced if stored or operated outside of these ambient temperature ranges. Avoid exposing your Apple Watch to remarkable changes in temperature or humidity. When the interior temperature of Apple smart Watch exceeds average operating temperatures (for instance, in scorching weather or direct sunlight for extended time), you may likely experience the following as the Apple smart operating capabilities attempt to regulate its temperature:

Charging may slow or stop.

1. The Apple display may dim.

2. A temperature-warning screen icon may appear.

3. Particular data transfer may be paused or delayed.

4. Some Apple apps may close.

It is crucial to know that you may not be able to use Apple Watch,. In contrast, the temperature warning screen is displayed.

Because, if Apple Watch can't regulate its internal ambient temperature, it usually goes into a power reserve or a deep sleep mode until it cools down. When this problem occurs, move your Apple smart Watch to a more relaxed location out of direct sunlight or hot car and wait a few minutes before trying to use it again.

It is essential to keep critical cards and credit cards away from Apple Watch, the bands, the Apple Watch magnetic charging cable, and the Apple Watch magnetic charging case.

Best Apple Watch bands

Who cares that someone has a solid gold Apple Watch band?. Now there are several popular options available — even some you can customize — your style will come shining through when you wear your new smartwatch, you won't need to spend $15,000 on the precious metal. These simple, well-designed, and chic watchband designs range from $16.00 to $250, and since Apple makes it easy to slide in and out new bands, you can have one to match any outfit.

Apple Milanese

The brand Milanese Loop band from Apple epitomizes modern swank while still evoking 19th-century Italian style. The stainless-steel mesh wraps around your wrist to magnetically close without any fumbling over clasps. Because it's substantially adjustable, this band should fit any wrist to perfection.

Apple watch leather loop

Add a few Italian luxuries to your Apple Watch with the company's $148 leather loop band. The band's Venezia leather has a unique, distressed look, and it comes in 4 muted-yet-chic colors: blue, black, brown, and taupe. It has a magnetic closure for secure fastening and removing the Apple Watch, and the closure is adjustable, so you can make it as tight if you wish or as loose as you want.

Apple watch woven Nylon Band

This woven nylon is durable yet still stylish, Apple's nylon bands are made from more than 500 colorful threads woven together in 4 layers for a fabric-like feel. The band comes in Light Pink/Midnight Blue, Yellow/Light Gray, Space Orange or Anthracite, Toasted Coffee or Caramel, and Nav Tahoe Blue.

Apple Modern Buckle

For the real Apple fan, the Midnight Blue Modern Buckle is a very stylish selection. The top-grain leather looks luxurious, while the two-piece magnetic closure of the buckle is exceptionally refined. The leather strap comes in black, brown, or pink as well, but the deep blue offers a subtle hint of cultivated style.

Coach Apple watch studs leather strap

Bring your Apple Watch to look back down to earth a bit with this Western-style, soft leather strap dotted with lacquered studs. Besides the pictured ginger version, the band comes in black, with both versions offering studs in olive, titanium, and a pearly white. Designed solely for women, this Coach band is sized only for the 38 mm Apple Watch.

Casetify customize Apple watch band

Most the do-it-yourselfers know the value of making amazing for themselves. With Casetify's Customized Apple Watch Band, you can do just that. Through the site, you can upload images, use emoji, or connect to your Instagram or Facebook account to grab photos to place on the watchband. Then, you can add one of 8 photo filters, such as sepia, to give the six pictures you choose a similar look.

Monowear Nylon Olive band with chrome loops

This Monowear Nylon Olive Band with Chrome Loops works best with the stainless-steel or silver-aluminum watch faces. The circles keep the surplus band from flapping around, while the rugged nylon material adds an air of funk and independence to the popular smartwatch.

Monowearable metal

While indistinctly reminiscent of the Apple Link Bracelet, the Monowear Black Metal is just a bit snazzier. Its stainless-steel structure is swath in a matte black color. This band is also available in either 38 mm or 42 mm for the Watch Sport, Watch Edition, or base Watch. It can be customized to adapt flawlessly with Apple's stainless-steel, aluminum, or space-gray watch faces.

Etsy Minimalist and Zen watch strap.

This is for those who love the refined look of leather and prefer a simple design, the Etsy Minimalist and Zen Watch Strap may be just the answer. Available in 38 mm or 42 mm, it's made of vegetable-tanned leather that will probably fade from yellow to brown over time; applying neatsfoot oil or mink oil will speed up this change. You can select a golden- or silver-Colore brass stud clasp.

How to care Apple Watchband

It is advisable to use only Apple-branded or Apple authorized bands. Clean the bands, remove the band from Apple Watch before cleaning.

But, for the leather part of the bands, wipe them clean with a nonabrasive, lint-free cloth, lightly dampened with water. After cleaning, allow the band air dry thoroughly before re-attaching it back to Apple Watch. You should not store leather bands in direct sunlight, at very high temperatures, or in high humidity. Furthermore, don't soak leather bands in freshwater. The leather bands are not water-resistant.

For other bands and clasps, wipe them clean with a nonabrasive, lint-free cloth, lightly dampened with water. Dry the band thoroughly with a nonabrasive, lint-free cloth before reattaching it back.

How to remove, change, and fasten bands

In this part, you will learn the general instructions for removing, changing, and fastening bands. All the time, ensure that you're replacing a band with a similar one of the same size. The bands are sized according to the size of Apple smart Watch and should not be just used interchangeably. Some band styles made specifically for a particular size Apple smart Watch only.

To change bands

Press the band release button on your Apple Watch, slide the band across to remove it, then slide the new band. Never force a new band into it's slot. However, if you're having difficulty removing or inserting a band, then press the band release button again.

The band release button

Fasten a band. For a more excellent performance, Apple smart Watch should fit tightly on your wrist. The back of Apple Watch needs good skin contact for features like wrist detection, haptic notifications, and the heart rate sensor. It is also another trick for wearing Apple smart Watch with the right fit-not too tight, not too loose, and with enough room for your skin to breathe. It may keep you more comfortable and let the sensors do their work. At times you may like to tighten Apple Watch for your workouts, then *loosen the band when you're done. Also, the device sensors will work only when you wear the Watch on the top of your wrist.*

CHAPTER 22

Apple Watch troubleshooting

*T*he team of our researchers compiled most familiar Apple watch problems and how to fix them. Apple watch series 4 is of the most accessible smartwatch on the market, but the watch does not always work correctly as it should be.

After comprehensive research, digging to find out comments, and gathering opinions on a watch issue, glitches, and everyday apple watch troubleshooting. These are selected most of the standard Apple Watch problems. If you've been suffering from one of the list problems, don't let that Apple Watch wind you up — we've got workarounds and possible fixes for you to try. We have dealt with almost all Apple watch problems and prosper their solutions professionally in this chapter.

Problem:1 light bleed on Apple watch s4 display

There are several discussions on light bleed from the Apple Watch Series 4 display. When you're in a dark environment, and the brightness dims, you may observe that one side of the Apple Watch display is brighter than the other and appears yellow. This isn't a genuinely light bleed, because the screen is an OLED, but rather it seems to be an issue with the gray image.

Solution;

There is no way to fix this yourself, so you need to

Prepare a replacement of a watch from Apple.

Problem 2; Glitch, messages remain unread on Apple watch series 4

We had a few people report an infuriating glitch where they read messages on their iPhone, nevertheless, those messages continue to appear as unread on their Apple Watch. This glitch mostly seems to be triggered more when people switch to a new iPhone

Solution;

Close the Message App on your iPhone, then switch both your iPhone and Apple Watch off by directly pressing and holding the power button, now sliding to power off. Finally, turn your iPhone back on first, then your Apple watch and sync accurately.

Problem 3; Screen has popped out of the Apple casing

Several sources have confirmed that the Apple Watch will occasionally experience an issue where the entire screen pops out of the watch's casing. This problem was recently identified by our researcher's survey, whereby Apple watch owners complained about this issue. It is believed that the issue stems from the battery. As Apple watches battery ages, it swells, taking up more space in Apple's small innards, and this forces the screen out.

This problem may likely persist as all models of the Apple Watch may suffer from this particular defect.

Solution

Take your Apple watch to the nearest Apple Store, or get contact with support. Because. Any fault that is battery-related, Apple will consider the warranty, which in most cases can be extended to three years to account for this kind of failure.

Problem 4; Apple watch won't connect to LTE

When there's this kind of issue that the LTE variant of the Apple Watch is already known for its problems connecting to cellular. Apple publicly accepted this issue and said that it would push a fix in an update back in Sept-Oct 2017. Apple did officially address the item in the WatchOS 4.0.1 update, clearing up that it had to do with the Apple Watch having problems with the hand-off between Wi-Fi and cellular. The update barred the Apple Watch from joining unauthenticated Wi-Fi networks. It was reported to fix the LTE connectivity issues for some people, although others are still waiting for LTE fix.

Solution

Update your Apple Watch software. Open the Apple Watch app on your iPhone and then go to General > Software Update. You may try to set up your cellular plan once again. Open the Apple watch app and go to My Watch tab, tab the I next to Carrier, and then Remove. You can also add your cellular plan again by tapping on Add a New Plan, reactivate it, and finally reboot the Apple Watch.

Problem 5; No iPhone connection error

Once turning the Apple Watch back on, or at times after using Airplane mode, the Apple Watch may give you a No iPhone error. If this happens, the best way to deal with it is to let your Apple Watch and iPhone find each other again.

Solution

Start by making sure that Airplane mode is turned off on both your Watch and iPhone, and that Wi-Fi and Bluetooth are turned on.

To restart your Apple watch, hold side button till you see Power off slider. Slide the Power off slider to the most right and when Apple is off, turn it back on just press and hold the side button until see the Apple logo.

To restart the iPhone X, press and hold the side button and one volume button until the Slide to power off slider appears. To reset the iPhone 8 or earlier, hold down the sleep/wake button until the Slide to power off slider appears. The sleep/wake button is located on the right side of the top if you have an iPhone 5s or earlier

If all these fail, you can always try to unpair the device and pair them again.

Problem 6; Bluetooth will not connect or frequently disconnect.

Solution

There are a pair of different possible glitches at play here. Some find that their Apple Watch will disconnect from their iPhone, even when they're in close range. Others complaint about having Bluetooth problems when they are trying to use their headphones for a workout. There are a few things you can do to get Bluetooth working again for workout

Proximity issues for Bluetooth and different devices have different proximity ranges. So stated that there is better performance after switching the device they were using the same side of their body as the Apple Watch.

If the problem is with Bluetooth headphones and music streaming, then sync your playlist onto your Apple Watch and turn Bluetooth on your iPhone off.

Solution

If the issue is with your iPhone then, turning an Airplane mode on your iPhones on and off. Alternatively, you may go to setting>Bluetooth and toggle it off, then wait for a few seconds and toggle it back again.

Press and hold the side button on Apple Watch till the slider appears, then drag Power off to the right.

To turn it back, hold down the side button until the Apple logo appears.

If the iPhone is giving you trouble, try unpairing.

The final resort is to erase all content and settings on Apple Watch. Go to setting> general>reset > Erase All content and Settings.when it is done, you can pair your Apple Watch iPhone.

Problem7; Apple watch poor battery performance

Apple watch battery life is one of the main weaknesses of the Apple Watch, but it should generally get you through the day before needing a refuel.

Solution

You can select to put Apple Watch in power reserve mode, and it only shows the time. Press *and hold the side button on your Apple Watch till the sliders appear, then drag power reserve to the right.*

Open up the Watch app on your iPhone and go into Notifications and turn off everything that you don't need.

Go to Setting>Brightness and text size on Apple Watch to reduce brightness.

On your Apple Watch, go Setting > General>Wake Screen and toggle off Wake Screen on Wrist Raise. You can do this in the Apple Watch app on your iPhone.

Problem 8; Apple Watch will not charge

If you find out that your Apple Watch won't charge up, then remember that it can take a few seconds for the charging icon to pop up on the screen when the Apple Watch is completely drained. Here's what you should check before you start to panic.

Solution

If your Apple Watch is brand new, then make sure that you do not have any plastics still attached to the Watch charger.

Use the Apple Magnetic Charging Cable and the USB Power Adapter that originally came with your Apple Watch.

Check that both surfaces are immaculate, and you can remove any case or anything else you might have on Apple Watch.

Try plugging the cable into a laptop, computer, or any other power adapter in a different socket.

Hold down the Watch side button and swipe Power off to the right

Digital Crown can behold down for at least ten seconds till you see the Apple Watch logo

The last is to try to open the Apple Watch app on your iPhone and Go to >General>Reset>Erase all Content and Setting

If all these not work, it the right time to contact Apple.

Problem 9; My Apple watch stopped working?

Solution

Position the back of your Apple Watch on the charger again. If your Watch still won't charge, force it to restart. Then press and hold both the side button and Digital Crown for 10 seconds, or until you see the Apple Watch logo. If the problem persists, try a different

Apple Watch Magnetic Charging Cable and USB Power Adapter.

Problem 10; How do you unfreeze an Apple watch?

Solution

Restarting Your Apple Watch. If your device is badly frozen and won't respond to the side button action, then press and hold both the side button and digital crown at the same time for about 10 second

Problem 11; How to reboot your Apple watch?

Solution

Restart your Apple Watch

Press and hold the side button pending you see the Power Off slider.

Drag the Power Off slider.

After your Apple watch turns off, press and hold the side button again until you see the Apple logo appear.

Problem 12; How do I fix my Apple watch from glitching?

Solution

Hold down the side button to turn it back on. But this might only be a temporary solution. When your Apple Watch is locked up and insensitive, try holding down the side button and the Digital Crown together for at least 10 seconds, until you see the Apple logo appear.

Problem 13; what happens if I reset my Apple Watch?

Solution

Go to general> Setting>Reset> Erase all content, then press Erase All you'll delete all of the data, and that'll reset your Apple Watch to its factory settings. Though, this won't unpair your Apple Watch from your account.

Problem 14; why my apple watch crown get stuck?

Solution

According to Apple expert, if the digital crown of your Apple Watch gets stuck or won't move, it could have dust or debris under, this can be fixed by running the Apple Watch under fresh water from a faucet for 10 to 15 seconds.

Problem 15; How do I fix my Apple Watch digital crown?

Solution

How to Fix the Digital Crown on your Apple Watch:

Turn off the Apple Watch and remove it from the charger.

If you have a leather band, remove it from your Apple Watch too.

Hold the Digital Crown under lightly running, warm, freshwater from a faucet for 10 seconds.

Problem 16; How do I turn water lock-off on Apple Watch?

Solution

When you finish the water-based workout, or anytime you want to turn off water lock, you'll need to use these steps.

Turn the Digital Crown.

Keep turning the Digital Crown until the Apple Watch says it's unlocked.

Problem 17; what is the water drop on Apple Watch?

Solution

The Apple Watch is made up of water resistant ability. This will automatically lock the screen to avoid water droplets from mimicking taps on the screen while you are in the water. The moment you get out of the water, you can turn the Digital Crown clockwise, and the Watch speaker will emit a series of sounds destined to push the water out of the speaker hole.

Problem 18; why is Apple Watch stuck on the Apple logo?

Solution

The first thing to do is to force your Apple watch stuck on the Apple logo to restart. For that, Press the holding button on your Apple watch at least for 10 seconds. By doing this diligently, you can come to the conclusion that the Apple watch may be stuck due to some software problems.

Problem 19; How to fix a stuck Apple Watch logo?

Solution

You can force restart your Apple Watch if it is stuck as you can force restart your iPhone. To force reboot the Apple Watch; all you have to do is press the digital crown and the side button simultaneously for 10 seconds. Then release both buttons when you see the Apple logo appear.

Problem 20; How do I reset my Apple watch without my phone?

Solution

How to unpair your Apple Watch directly on the smartwatch

Open the Settings app on your Apple Watch.

Then tap on the General setting.

Select Reset.

Tap on Erase All Content and Settings.

Type in your passcode (if enabled).

Tap on Erase All (or, if you have, a cellular plan and wish to keep it, Erase All & Keep Plan).

CHAPTER 23

Apple watches more questions and answers.

Problem 21; How do I completely reset my Apple Watch?

Solution

Use your paired iPhone

Keep the Apple Watch and iPhone close together until you complete these steps.

Open the Apple Watch app and tap the My Watch tab.

Then tap General > Reset.

Tap Erase Apple Watch Content and Settings, then finally tap again to confirm.

Problem 22; How do I do a tough reset on my Apple Watch?

Solution

To force restart the Apple Watch, press and hold both the side button and Digital Crown for 10 seconds, then release both buttons when you see the Apple logo appear.

Problem 23; Should I turn my Apple watch off?

Solution

The watch face appears when Apple Watch is on. Turn off: As a rule, you'll leave your Apple Watch on all of the time, but if you like to turn it off, press and hold the side button until the sliders appear, then drag the Power Off slider to the right.

Problem 24; How do I repair my Apple Watch?

Solution

If your Apple Watch can't connect, unpair your devices, then pair them again:

On your Apple Watch, tap Settings > General > Reset > Erase All Content and Settings

Also, on your iPhone, open the Apple Watch app, tap the My Watch tab, then tap your watch at the top of the screen. ...

Pair your Apple Watch and iPhone again.

Problem 25; Can I fix Apple watch screens?

Solution

The Apple Watch warranty doesn't cover damage caused by accident or abuse. The concluding cost to serve an accidentally damaged screen depends on your Apple Watch model, any additional damage, and if you have AppleCare+ coverage. If you have

AppleCare+, it covers up to two incidents of any accidental damage.

Problem 26; What is theater mode on Apple Watch?

Solution

First introduced in watch OS 3.2, Theater Mode is an accessible but handy feature that's designed to prevent the Apple Watch's screen from activating when you raise your wrist.

Problem 27; How do I reset my Apple watch with too many passcode attempts?

Solution

While keeping the Watch on the charger and connected to power:

Press and hold the side button until you notice the Power Off slider.

Press firmly on Power Off, but do not try to slide it - press down more securely than a normal tap, release your finger and then tap on Erase all content and settings and confirm.

Problem 28; Can I shower with my Apple Watch 2?

Solution

Showering with the version of Apple Watch Series 2, Apple Watch Series 3, and Apple Watch Series 4 is ok, but I recommend not exposing Apple Watch to soaps, shampoos, conditioners, lotions, and perfumes as they can harmfully affect water seals and acoustic membranes.

Problem 29; Can I use a stolen Apple Watch?

Solution

So if your watch is accidentally lost or stolen, you can use Find My iPhone to help you find it again. Apple Watch Series 4(GPS) and Apple Watch Series 3 and 2 can use GPS and a trusted Wi-Fi connection. Because Apple Watch Series 1 doesn't have GPS, you'll see the location of your paired iPhone or its Wi-Fi connection.

Problem 30; How do I unstick my Apple Watch crown?

Solution

There are three ways on which Unstick a Sticky Digital Crown on your Apple Watch

Turn off your Apple Watch and remove it from the charger.

If you have a leather band, remove it from your Apple Watch.

Hold the Digital Crown under lightly running, warm, freshwater from a faucet for 10 seconds.

Problem 31; why does my Apple watch say turn the digital crown to unlock and eject water.

Solution

To turn off Water Lock on the Apple Watch, which is what you are describing, keep turning the Digital Crown until the water droplet fills the circle, and your Apple Watch states Unlocked (you can also hear the speaker make sounds.

Problem 32; How do you remove a stuck Apple watch band?

Solution

Make sure to hold down the release oval, so the band doesn't get stuck. Do again on the opposite end of a watch to remove the second band. Take the new band. Ensure that the underside of the band is facing you and slide until you feel it click into place.

Problem 33; How do I unstick my Apple Watch button?

Solution

Turn off you're the Watch and remove it from the charger. If you have a leather band, remove it from your Apple Watch. Hold the Digital Crown under lightly running, warm, freshwater from a faucet for 10 seconds.

Problem 34; How do you remove water from Apple Watch?

Solution

To get all the water or sweat out of the Apple Watch speaker, you need to take advantage of your Apple Watch's built-in water ejection feature. On the Apple watch face, swipe up from the bottom of the screen to open the Control Center. Scroll down until you see the water drop icon.

Problem 35; What does turn the digital crown mean?

Solution

The Digital Crown is Apple's answer to the crown originates on mechanical watches. Historically, the crown is used to set the date and time on any wristwatch, and to wind the mainspring to keep the watch running. Apple

Watch users can press the Digital Crown to go back to the Home screen, much like the home button on an iPhone.

Problem 36; Does Apple watch need water lock?

Solution

The Apple Watch Series 2 and 3 enable Water lock automatically when starting a Swimming workout. To manually remove water from Apple Watch, swipe up on the bottom of the watch face to open Control Center, tap Water Lock, then turn the Digital Crown to unlock the screen and clear water from the speaker.

Problem 37; Can Apple Watch 3 get wet?

Solution

Apple Watch Series 3 is also water- and dust-resistant. Like the Series 2, the Apple

Watch Series 3 is hermetically sealed. You can shower with the watch and swim with it in pools and the ocean, though at only shallow depths.

Problem 38; Can Apple Watch 4 get wet?

Solution

Your Apple Watch loves getting wet. But when you start a swimming workout, the waterproof mode kicks in automatically, that is means the Apple Watch touch screen stops working.

Problem 39; How do I turn off activation lock on Apple Watch?

Solution

On your computer, go to iCloud.com and sign in with your Apple ID.

Go to Find My iPhone.

Select All Devices, and then click your Apple Watch.

Click Erase Apple Watch. Select Next until the device is erase.

Click next to your Apple Watch.

Problem 40; How do you troubleshoot Apple Watch?

Solution

To restart your Watch, follow these steps:

Press and hold the side button until the digital switches appear.

Slide the Power Off switch to the right to turn off your Apple Watch.

To restart the Watch once it turns off, hold down the side button until you see the Apple logo appear.

CHAPTER 24

Maintenance of Apple Watch

To keep your valuable Apple watch, you need to masters the maintenance tips. So we need to revise this vital information. Always keep your Apple Watch clean and dry. Clean and dry Apple smart Watch, the band, and your skin following workouts or profound sweating.

Dry Apple Watch face and the band meticulously if they are exposed to freshwater. Clean Apple Watch if exposed to everything that may cause stains, or other damage, such as dirt, sand, makeup, ink, soap, detergent, acid solution, or acidic foods. Or when comes in contact with liquids other than water, including those that may lead to skin irritation like sweat, saltwater, soapy water, pool water, perfume, insect repellent, lotions, sunscreen, oil. Others are adhesive remover, hair dye, or solvents, etc. Despite the regular care, the Apple Watch and band colors may vary or fade over a period.

Turn off Apple Watch.

Press and hold the side button of your Watch, then drag the Power Off slider to the right.

Then depress the band release buttons and remove the band.

Wipe Apple Watch, clean with a nonabrasive, lint-free cloth. You may also lightly dampen the cloth with fresh water.

Dry Apple Watch with a lint-free, nonabrasive cloth.

Apple Watch (gold) models benefit the most if you clean them frequently. Clean with a nonabrasive, lint-free cloth to get rid of surface oil, perfumes, lotions, and other substances, particularly before storing the Apple Watch.

These things not recommended in the care of your Apple Smart Watch:

1. Do not clean Apple Watch at the same time as it's charging.

2. Do not dry Apple Watch, the bands using an external heat source like a hair dryer.

3. Do not use chemical cleaning products or compressed air when cleaning your Apple Watch.

The front of Apple Watch is made by Ion-X glass or sapphire crystal, each with a fingerprint-resistant oleophobic, which is oil-repellent coating substances. This coating material wears over time with regular usage. Cleaning products and abrasive substances will further diminish the coating, and may probably scratch the glass or the sapphire crystal.

You should never apply excessive pressure to a button or the Digital Crown on Apple Watch, or to force a charging connector into its port, for the reason that, this may cause damage that is not cover under the company warranty. Take note that if the connector and port don't join with reasonable ease, most likely, they don't match.

Check for any obstruction and make sure that the connector matches the port and that you have placed the connector correctly in relation to the port.

Some specific usage patterns can be a factor in the fraying or breaking of cables. The cable attached to a charging component, like any other metal cable, is subject to becoming brittle or weak if repetitively bent in the same spot. It will be prevented by gentle curves instead of angles in the cable. Regularly, inspect the cable and connector for any kinks, breaks, bends, or any damage. In case you find any such damage, discontinue the use of the cable.

It is normal after regular use the lightning connector to USB cable can get discoloration. Extreme dirt, debris, and exposure to moisture may cause discoloration. If your lightning cable or connector becomes so warm during use or if Apple Watch won't charge, disconnect the cable from the power adapter and clean the lightning connector with a non-corrosive, dry, lint-free cloth. You should not use liquids or cleaning agents when cleaning the Lightning connector.

Magnetic charging cable and magnetic charging case

The Apple Watch magnetic charging cable and magnetic charging case discoloration of the charging surface may occur after regular use due to dirt and debris that come in contact with the magnetic surface. This is common.

Cleaning the magnetic charging surface may reduce, or prevent, that discoloration, and will help to avoid damage to your charger and Apple smart Watch. if you want to clean the charging surface, disconnect the charger from both Apple Watch and the power adapter outlets and wipe with a damp, nonabrasive lint-free cloth. Always dry it with a nonabrasive, lint-free cloth before charging again. This also not requires using a cleaning chemical agent when cleaning the charging surface.

Apple Watch normal temperature

Apple Watch operating temperature is designed to work best in ambient temperatures between 0° and 35°C and be stored in temperatures between -20° and 45° C. Apple Watch can be spoiled and battery life reduced if stored or operated outside of these ambient temperature ranges. Avoid exposing your Apple Watch to remarkable changes in temperature or humidity. When the interior temperature of Apple smart Watch exceeds average operating temperatures (for instance, in scorching weather or direct sunlight for an extended period of time), you may likely experience the following as the Apple smart operating capabilities attempt to regulate its temperature:

Charging may slow or stop.

1. The Apple display may dim.

2. A temperature-warning screen icon may appear.

3. Certain data transfer may be paused or delayed.

4. Some Apple apps may close.

It is vital to know that you may not be able to use Apple Watch, whereas the temperature warning screen is displayed. Because, if Apple Watch can't regulate its internal ambient temperature, it usually goes into a power reserve or a deep sleep mode until it cools down. When this problem occurs, move your Apple smart Watch to a more relaxed location out of direct sunlight or hot car and wait a few minutes before trying to use it again.

It is very essential to keep key cards and credit cards away from Apple Watch, the bands, the Apple Watch magnetic charging cable, and the Apple Watch magnetic charging case.

How to care Apple Watchband

It is advisable to use only Apple-branded or Apple authorized bands. Clean the bands, remove the band from Apple Watch before cleaning.

But, for the leather part of the bands, wipe them clean with a nonabrasive, lint-free cloth, lightly dampened with water. After cleaning, allow the band air dry thoroughly before re-attaching it back to Apple Watch. You should not store leather bands in direct sunlight, at very high temperatures, or in high humidity. Furthermore, don't soak leather bands in freshwater. The leather bands are not water-resistant.

For other bands and clasps, wipe them clean with a nonabrasive, lint-free cloth, lightly dampened with water. Dry the band thoroughly with a nonabrasive, lint-free cloth before reattaching it back.

How to remove, change, and fasten bands

In this part, you will learn the general instructions for removing, changing, and fastening bands. All the time ensure that you're replacing a band with a similar one of the same size.

The bands are sized according to the size of Apple smart Watch and should not be just used interchangeably. Some band styles made specifically for a particular size Apple smart Watch only.

To change bands

Press the band release button on your Apple Watch, slide the band across to remove it, then slide the new band. Never force a new band into its slot. However, if you're having difficulty removing or inserting a band, then press the band release button again.

The band release button

Fasten a band. For more excellent performance, Apple smart Watch should fit tightly on your wrist. The back of Apple Watch needs good skin contact for features *like wrist detection, haptic notifications, and the heart rate sensor. It is also another trick for wearing Apple smart Watch with the right fit-not too tight, not too loose, and with enough room for your skin to breathe. It may keep you more comfortable and let the sensors do their work. At times you may like to tighten Apple Watch for your workouts, then loosen the band when you finish. Also, the device sensors will work when you wear the Watch on the top of your wrist.*

CHAPTER 25

Apple Watch, the Doctor on Your Wrist

*J*ames David thought he had a panic attack. He took a break from work to walk around the block during a stressful day and noticed he felt out of breath, strolling up a slight incline. It isn't healthy, James thought. He had become an enthusiastic cycler in recent months and wasn't exactly out of shape. He sat down at his desk and looked at the Apple Watch series on his wrist.

His heart rate was very high, and the Apple Watch ECG app he was using to check his pulse was flashing warnings. Maybe it was a bit more serious, he thought.

Although he had a pulmonary embolism two years back. He had been on medication, and doctors said that it was an unusual condition for somebody in their mid-20s. Still, the *symptoms this time were much less severe, and he was feeling stressed, so his mind didn't automatically jump to blood clots. James's doctor told him it sounded like acute anxiety. Then he showed him a log of his heart rate recorded by the Apple Watch ECG app.*

"This is my normal heart rate," James told him, pointing to the graph in the app. "This is where my heart is now. There's something wrong." The doctor ordered a CT scan. The CT scan result indicates blood clots in his left lung had returned.

An ambulance rushed James to the emergency room, where he was pumped full of blood thinners. He didn't need surgery this time, but doctors told him that if he had waited, a clot could have killed him. James isn't the only person who has discovered a serious health condition after seeing heart-rate data on an Apple smartwatch. And he won't be the last.

How Apple watches are saving Lives

I was worried when I opened the ECG app for the first time on the Apple Watch Series 4.

I have no known heart issues. I'm a strict disciplinarian about regular physicals. But I had never been to any cardiologist or had an electrocardiogram. And I was a little frightened that the Apple Watch might notify me of something about my health that I didn't know. I wasn't confident I even wanted to know. Nevertheless, when I got early access to the ECG app, which officially rolls out to my Apple watch series four on Thursday, Dec. 24, 2018, I had to make an effort for myself.

I pressed my right forefinger touching the watch's Digital Crown and held it there for 30 seconds as the watch measured my heart rhythm, but trying not to catch my breath at the same time. I watched my heartbeat graphed in real-time on the Apple watch screen, trying to interpret on my own if it was normal. It seemed reasonable, but I'm no professional about it — the result displays: Sinus Rhythm. No atrial fibrillation detected. I clenched my fist in the air, realizing that I had been a little concerned.

Preferably, you'll never need to use the Apple Watch's ECG app. Except if you feel something strange, a fluttering in your chest or your pulse. You can take what's similar to a clinical single-lead electrocardiogram directly on your wrist using an Apple watch. It could be a very important lifesaver. ECG and EKG are both abbreviations for an electrocardiogram, which measures the electrical activity of the heart. Doctors and other health professionals often refer to it as an EKG; Apple's watch app called it ECG.

What you need to know about ECG

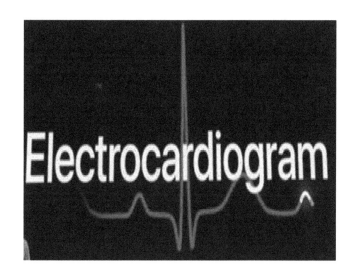

Electrocardiography is the scientific procedure by which electrical activities of the heart are analyzed and studied. The spread of excitation through heart muscle myocardium produces a local electrical potential. This low-intensity current flows throughout a body, which acts as a volume conductor.

This current can be picked up from a surface of the body by using appropriate electrodes and recorded in the form of an electrocardiogram. The technique firstly discovered by Dutch physiologists. Einthoven Willem who considered as the father of electrocardiogram (ECG).

Electrocardiograph

The electrocardiograph is the medical device by which the electrical activities of the heart are analyzed and recorded.

Electrocardiogram

Electrocardiogram derives from electrocardiogram in Dutch EKG, or ECG is the graphical record of electrical activities of the heart, which occur before the onset of mechanical activities. It is the sum of the electrical activity of cardiac muscle fibers, recorded from the surface of the body.

General functions of ECG

The electrocardiogram is very useful in determining and diagnosing the following heart parameters.

1. Heart rate

2. Heart rhythm

3. Abnormal electrical conduction

4. Inadequate blood supply to the heart muscle (ischemia)

5. Heart attack

6. Heart coronary artery disease

7. Hypertrophy of heart chambers.

ECG GRID

The paper used for recording ECG is called ECG paper.ECG device amplifies the electrical signals produced from the heart and records these signals on a moving ECG paper.

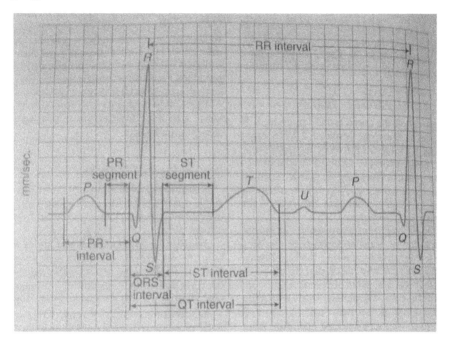

The electrocardiographic grid refers to the markings lines on ECG paper. ECG paper has horizontal and vertical lines at regular intervals of 1 mm each. Every 5th line (5mm)is bolded.

Time duration

The time duration of different ECG waves is usually plotted horizontally on X-axis.

On X-axis

1 mm = 0.04 second

5 mm = 0.20 second

Amplitude

An amplitude of ECG waves is plotted vertically on Y-axis.

On Y-axis

1 mm = 0.1 mV

5 mm = 0.5 mV

The speed of the paper

The movement of the paper through the machine can be adjusted by two rates, 25 mm/second and 50 mm/second. Frequently, the speed of the paper during recording set at 25 mm/second. If the heart rate is very high, an acceleration of the paper changed to 50 mm/second.

CHAPTER 26

How the ECG App Works

*T*he Apple Watch cannot identify heart attacks, high blood pressure, blood clots, or any condition aside from atrial fibrillation. Which is an irregular heart rhythm that can be, but isn't necessarily, related to those heart issues?

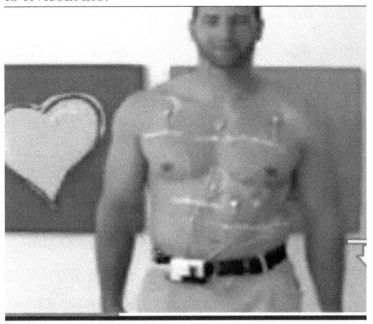

My watch told me I was in Sinus Rhythm multiple times, and I believed it. But to ensure everything is alright, I subjected myself to a 12 lead electrocardiogram in a hospital, at least, for science. Like the Apple Watch's ECG, a full EKG takes just 30 seconds. The ECG app's results are not comparable to a 12-lead EKG, because the watch's sensor is similar to a single lead, measuring a

single point on the body. To be more precise, Apple does not advocate comparing the two, because they are not the same. A 12-lead EKG can be used to diagnose an array of issues, including heart attacks. A single-lead ECG cannot do that.

My physician attached 12 leads to my body across my chest, arms, and legs — to measure the electrical pulses from head to toe. Each point reveals different information, but it is likely to diagnose atrial fibrillation from a single lead. You can also measure high and low heart rate from one edge, but that's about it.

My full EKG finally confirmed that my heart rhythm is indeed normal; no atrial fibrillation detected. Wow. I tried simultaneously undergoing the EKG and taking a measurement in the Apple ECG app, but due to the electrical interference resulted in a noisy reading.

We also learn that last years, during the world cup, most of the England fans warned about their heart rates during a tense penalty shootout.

Apple Watches warned England fans that there could be something seriously wrong with their hearts during the team's penalty shootout against Colombia. The stress of watching the game sent pulses rocketing among fans forced to watch their team fight to stay in the World Cup. Imagine!

Apple Watch for heart diseases detection

With the accessibility of watch OS 5.1.2 and Apple Watch Series 4, which incorporated with ECG capability. Apple Watch customers nowadays have access to two features to detect heart problems such as arrhythmias and atrial fibrillation. Apple Watch Series 1, 2, and 3 can look for arrhythmias using a photoplethysmograph based algorithm. But, the ECG app on Apple Watch Series 4 is capable of generating an ECG similar to a Lead I electrocardiogram. This app also classifies an ECG as sinus rhythm (SR), atrial fibrillation (AF), or inconclusive, and reports a high or low heart rate. This book is intended to provide a more detailed understanding of the capabilities of these features, including testing and validation.

The Atrial fibrillation

Atrial fibrillation is a type of irregular heart rhythm in which the upper heart chamber called atria.

Beat irregularly and sometimes rapidly is one of the leading causes of stroke. Although AF is often asymptomatic, leading many persons with AF to be unacquainted with this condition. The mix of stroke risk, no symptom presentation, effective pharmacologic treatments are reducing stroke risk. And increasing market infiltration of consumer devices with the potential to discover AF have increased much interest in the early detection of AF outside the clinical setting.

The watchOS 5.1.2, Apple Watch Series 1, 2and 3 are capable of identifying periods of irregular pulse suggestive of AF using photoplethysmograph (PPG) signals jointly with an algorithm. In addition to this PPG-based detection algorithm. Apple Watch Series 4 has an electrical heart sensor that, when using the ECG app, enables the generation and study of an ECG similar to a Lead I ECG.

Scientific description

Apple Watch has a unique optical heart sensor that uses green LED lights at the back surface to paired with light-sensitive photodiodes to detect blood pulses in a user's wrist using Photoplethysmography (PPG). These sensors and essential algorithms are the basis for the heart rate, and heart rate variability (HRV) detection enabled on Apple Watch Series 1 and rest.

For determination of HRV, Apple Watch captures a tachogram, a plot of the time linking heartbeats every 2 to 4 hours. Beginning with watch OS 5.1.2, a user may choose to enable an arrhythmia detection aspect that utilizes these echograms. To use the Irregular Rhythm Notification feature on Apple Watch, a user must initial complete onboarding within the Health app on the user's paired iPhone. To learn how to use the feature and receive tutoring regarding AF.

When the PPG-based arrhythmia detection is enabled, each tachogram is classified utilizing a proprietary algorithm to determine if an irregular rhythm may be present. An irregular tachogram initiates a surge of more frequent tachogram collection (as often as possible, subject to a bare minimum spacing of 15 minutes) and analysis.

Tachograms are collected and analyzed if the user remains at rest to obtain another reading. Because of this, the algorithm is not constantly monitoring the user, but to a certain extent, is doing so opportunistically when an adequate signal is available for collection/analysis. If 5 out of 6 sequential three tachograms (including the initial one) are classified as irregular within 48 hours, the user is notified of the possible arrhythmia. In addition to the arrhythmia notification, the user can also access more information related to these irregular tachograms within the Health app

If two tachograms are classified as not irregular before the threshold is reached, the cycle is automatically reset. And tachogram collection returns to the baseline rate (every 2 hours).

Preclinical development test

Preceding to the clinical testing, numerous studies were conducted to build up the PPG-based detection algorithm and to evaluate algorithm performance across a diversity of environmental conditions and user behaviors. Among these were regular sleeping, deep breathing, riding in a car, hand tremors, and motion. Reduced hand and wrist perfusion, overnight wear rapid ventricular response in those with AF and other arrhythmias. These studies were performed in 2500 control subjects and more than 600 people with AF.

Because PPG relies on LED light absorptivity, the arrhythmia detection algorithm tested across different types of skin and tones. To ensure that sense platform adjustments for skin tone were adequate in the framework of the algorithms used to detect arrhythmias. The skin contains Melanin that has high absorptivity at the wavelength used by the green LED on the Apple smartwatch — making PPG heart rate measurement potentially more complex in darker skin tones. Rectify this, the Apple Watch sensing platform adjusts LED current and thus light output, photodiode gain (sensitivity to emitted light), and sampling rate . To ensure adequate signal amplitude across all types of human skin tones.

In the Apple watch Health app, users can see the times when the algorithm identified an irregular tachogram that contributed to a notification on the (left).

Selecting one of these specific dates or times allows a user to visualize the beat-to-beat measurements calculated from both tachogram.

Health App View of Irregular Rhythm Measurements For validation purposes, 1.4 million tachograms from 1134 subjects (52% female) with varying skin type and tone (Fitzpa trick skin type and spectrophotometer-measured skin lightness at the wrist) were studied and analyzed.

The primary manufacturing concerns focused on signal amplitudes in persons with dark skin, nearly 5% of enrolled subjects had Fitzpatrick type VI skin, about twice the expected prevalence in the United States population.

The Validation efforts confirmed no significant difference in algorithm sensitivity or specificity across skin types/tones.

Clinical Validation from Apple Heart Study

The Apple Heart Study center (AHS), is a forthcoming single-arm pragmatic study conducted virtually, to evaluate the ability of the Apple Watch. Base irregular pulse notification algorithm to identify arrhythmia suggestive of AF. Contained by AHS, if a user met the requirement of a 5/6 irregular tachogram threshold, the user received an Apple Watch and iPhone notification. You had the option of contacting a telehealth physician and sent an ambulatory ECG patch. Participants instructed to wear the ePatch for up to one week; however, data collected from a participant were considered adequate with a minimum analyzable time of two hours.

Apple Watch ECG Description

Apple Watch Series 4 comes to a titanium electrode in their digital crown and an ultra-thin chromium silicon -carbon nitride layer applied to the sapphire crystal on the back of the Apple Watch. The ECG app detects and records the electrical impulses that control the heart from the user's fingertip on a digital crown and the wrist on the back of the Apple Watch. Which normally creates a short closed circuit. For using the ECG app on Apple Watch, a user must initially complete onboarding within the Health and fitness app on the user's paired iPhone to learn more on how to use the element and receive instruction regarding AF. To make an ECG, a user must open the ECG app installed on Apple Watch, then apply a finger from the hand contralateral to the wrist of the side where Apple Watch is worn to the digital crown for 30 seconds. Lead I polarity determined by the wrist placement of Apple Watch that already selected in Settings.

After obtaining the ECG, an algorithm is used to classify the ECG tracing as Sinus Rhythms (SR), atrial fibrillation (AF), or inconclusive.

This rhythms classification, on average heart rate, user-reported symptoms, and waveform are all stored in HealthKit and can be sent by the user as a PDF file from the Health app on the user's paired iPhone to the physicians.

The Apple Watch was publicly a remarkable event on September 9, 2014, in Cupertino at the Flint Center. It is the renowned symbolic place where Steve Jobs introduced the first Macintosh in 1984 and iMac in 1998, respectively.

After presenting a sequence of their new products and services, The current Apple CEO Tim Cook abruptly came back on stage with the memorable Steve Job's signature, and he says, "One more thing…".

It was the first tribute to the death of Jobs, a sign that the company was at last willing to let the Jobs legacy lie. He then introduced the most personal device Apple has ever created in the history of humankind.

Apple initial released in April 2015 its new line of product in three collections: Apple

Watch, Apple Watch Sport, and Apple Watch Edition. The company described the products on as follows:

The (Apple watch) collection features highly polished stainless steel and space black stainless steel cases. The face display protected by sapphire crystal. And there's a choice of three unique leather bands, a link bracelet, a Milanese loop, and a band made from the high-performance fluoro-elastomer component.

Conditions of functionality

The brand of Apple watch runs a version of iOS, different from its smartphone counterpart, but is not make calls from the watch without being connected to a compatible Apple smartwatch. But other vital functions are available such as notifications, activity, Siri, Apple Pay, etc.

Indications for use

The ECG app is an Apple watch software for only mobile medical applications intended for use with the Apple Watch series to create, record, store, transfer, and display a single-channel electrocardiogram (ECG) similar to a Lead I ECG of the standard lead I, II, and III.

The ECG app can determine the incidence of atrial fibrillation (AF) or sinus rhythm on a classifiable waveform. But the Apple Watch ECG app is not suggested for users with other known typical arrhythmias.

The ECG app is intended for over-the-counter (OTC) use only. The data displayed by the Apple Watch ECG app is designed for information exclusively. The user is not expected to interpret or take any clinical action based on the Apple Watch app output without consultation of a qualified healthcare professional.

The ECG waveform is intended to supplement rhythm classification to discriminate AF from typical normal sinus rhythm and not intended to replace conventional methods of diagnosis or treatment. The Apple ECG app is also not applicable to people under the age of 22.

CHAPTER 27

Using the ECG App

ECG Set-Up

*T*he ECG app is available on Apple Watch Series 4 with watch OS 5.1.2 and series 5 generation, paired with iPhone 5s or later with iOS 12.1.1.

•*Open the Health app on your iPhone.*

•*on the Health Data tab, tap Heart, then select "Electrocardiogram (ECG)"*

•*Follow the screen instructions.*

•You may exit on-boarding at any time by pressing "Cancel."

Recording an Apple ECG

•Ensure your Apple Watch is snug on the wrist you selected in Settings > General > Watch Orientation.

•Open the ECG app on your Apple smart Watch.

•Rest your arms on your lap or in the table, and hold your finger on the Digital Crown. No need to press the crown during the session.

•The recording takes almost 30 seconds.

Apple watches ECG Analysis.

•After a successful reading, you will receive one of the following classifications notifications on your ECG app:

1. *Sinus Rhythm: A normal sinus rhythm result means the heart is beating in a uniform pattern between 50-100 BPM.*

2. *Atrial Fibrillation: An AF result means the heart is beating in an irregular pattern between 50-120 BPM.*

3. *Inconclusive: An inconclusive result means that the recording can't be well classified. It can occur for reasons, like not resting your arms on a table during a record, or Apple Watch is too loosen your wrist. Some physiological conditions may prevent a small percentage of Apple users from creating enough signals to produce a good recording result.*

4. *Low or High Heart Rate: A heart rate under 50 BPM (beat per minute) or over 120 BPM affects the ECG app's capability to*

check for AF, and the recording is considered inconclusive.

After an Apple watch ECG recording is complete, the ECG data is analyzed to establish if it is at least 25 seconds long, and, if so, if either Sinus Rhythm or AF is present, or if an Inconclusive result is acceptable.

The ECG recording result on the ECG app provides a detailed display of the result. A comprehensive explanation will also provide on your iPhone.

The presence of AF in your ECG results may represent only potential findings. If you are experiencing any symptoms, contact your physician. If you believe you are experiencing any medical emergency, you should contact emergency services.

When it displays a result of Sinus Rhythm, it means that your heart rate is between 50 and 100 beats per minute and is beating in a uniform pattern and within normal ranges.

But when it displays inconclusive, ECG results mean that there may have been too much artifact or noise to acquire a high-quality signal. Or you may have an arrhythmia other than AF the app cannot classify, or your heart rate is between 100 and 120 BPM.

A small percentage of people may have specific physiological conditions preventing the user from getting enough signal to produce a good result.

You may learn more about Inconclusive ECG results during onboarding, by accessing more information in the ECG area of the Health app on your iPhone, or by tapping the "i" icon on the Apple ECG app for further details.

A heart rate under normal circumstances may be low because of certain medications or if electrical signals are not properly conducted through the heart muscle. Exercise training to be an athlete can also lead to a low heart rate.

A heart rate may be high because of exercise, stress, nervousness, alcohol dehydration, infection, AF, or other arrhythmias.

If you receive Inconclusive notifications result due to a poor recording, you might try to re-record your ECG. You can also review how to take an ECG during on-boarding or by tapping on

"Take a Recording" in the ECG area of the Health app on the iPhone.

All ECGs are synced to the Health app on your iPhone. You can use the Health app to share your ECG with a clinician.

The safety and performance of Apple watch ECG.

The Apple ECG app's ability to accurately classify an ECG recording into AF and normal sinus rhythm was extensively tested in a clinical trial of approximately 600 subjects.

The rhythm classification of a 12 standard lead ECG by a cardiologist was compared to the rhythm classification of a concurrently collected ECG from the Apple ECG app. The Apple ECG app established 98.3% sensitivity in classifying AF and 99.6% specificity in classifying sinus rhythm in classifiable recordings.

In this clinical trial, about 12.2% of recordings were inconclusive and not classifiable as either normal sinus rhythm or

AF. When inconclusive records were included in the analysis, the Apple ECG app correctly classified sinus rhythm in 90.5% of subjects with sinus rhythm and AF in 85.2% of subjects with AF. The clinical data validation results reflect use in a controlled environment. Real-world use of the Apple ECG app, can result in a more significant number of strips being deemed inconclusive and not classifiable.

The morphology of the waveform tested in this clinical trial by visual assessment of the standard PQRST wave and R wave amplitude in comparison to a reference. There was a tremendous success during this clinical trial; no adverse events are observed.

CHAPTER 28

Apple watches ECG troubleshooting.

If you get trouble in operating your Apple ECG app, below are some of the possible problems and their solutions.

1. Problem: I cannot get the ECG app to take my reading.

Solution :

• Make sure that you have completed all of the onboarding steps in the Health app on your iPhone.

• *Ensure your wrist and your Apple Watch are clean and dry. Water and sweat may cause a poor recording.*

• *Make sure that your Apple Watch, arms, and hands remain fixed during recordings.*

2. Problem: I have a lot of artifact, noise, or interference in the recording.

Solution:

• *Rest your arms on your lap or the table while you take a recording. Endeavor to relax and not move too much.*

• *Ensure your Apple Watch isn't loose on your wrist. The band should be tightly snug, and the back of your Apple Watch needs to be touching your wrist.*

• *Move away from all electronics that are plugged into an outlet to avoid electrical interference.*

3. Problem: The ECG waveforms appear upside down instead of upright.

Solution:

• The watch orientation may probability set to the wrong wrist. On your iPhone, go to the Watch app. Tap My Watch>General> Watch Orientation.

All data recorded during an Apple ECG app session saved to Health app on your iPhone. If you like, you can share that information by creating a PDF.

You should take note that new ECG data cannot record once your Apple Watch's storage is full. If you are not able to make a recording due to storage space issues, you should free up some space by deleting unwanted apps, music. You can check storage usage capacity, by navigating to the Apple Watch app on your iPhone, tapping "My

Watch," tapping "General," and then tapping "Usage."

The Apple ECG app cannot check for signs of an impending heart attack. If you believe you have a medical emergency, call emergency services.

Do not take recordings when Apple Watch is in close neighborhood to strong electromagnetic fields (e.g., electromagnetic anti-theft systems, metal detectors).

Do not take recordings during medical procedures such as magnetic resonance imaging. You are using diathermy, lithotripsy, cautery, and external defibrillation.

Do not take recordings when Apple Watch is outside of the operational optimum temperature range (0 oC – 35oC) and humidity of 20 % to 95% relative humidity.

As indicated in the similar author book named. Apple Watch (Series 4, 2019 Edition) The ultimate user guide, How to master Apple Watch in 2 Hours.

Don't of Apple watch ECG

Do not use it to diagnose heart-related conditions.

Do not use it with a cardiac pacemaker, ICDs, or other implanted electronic devices.

Do not take a recording during active physical activity.

Do not change your medication without consulting your doctor.

You should talk to your physicians if your heart rate is below 50 or over 120 when at rest and because this is an unexpected result.

You should also take note that interpretations made by this Apple watch app are potential findings, not a complete diagnosis of cardiac conditions. The user is not intended to guide clinical action based on the app outpour without consultation of a qualified healthcare professional.

The waveform generated by the Apple ECG app is only meant to supplement rhythm classification to discriminate AF from normal sinus rhythm and not intended to replace conventional methods of diagnosis or treatment.

Apple does not fully guarantee that you are not experiencing an arrhythmia or other health conditions when the Apple ECG app labels an ECG as Sinus Rhythm. You should instead notify your physician if you detect possible changes in your health.

Security tips

Apple recommends that you should add a passcode (personal identification number [PIN]), Face ID, or Touch ID (fingerprint)

to your iPhone and a passcode . (personal identification number [PIN]) to your Apple Watch to add more layers of security.

It is vital to secure your iPhone since you will be storing personal health information.

CHAPTER 29

Standard ECG components

*T*he standard ECG provides 12 different vectors that view the heart electrics activity. By convention, the ECG tracing is divide into P wave, PR interval. The QRS complex, QT interval, ST segment, T wave, and U wave. We are going to discuss the component very briefly here.

The p wave represents atrial depolarization. It is upright in most leads except AvR.

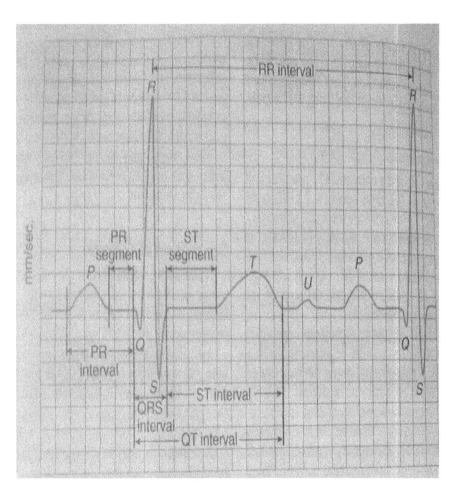

Normal ECG reading

It may be biphasic in lead II and Vi. The first component represents the right atrial activity, and 2 component represents left atrial activity. An increase in the amplitude of either or both parts occur with atrial enlargement. Right atrial enlargement produces a P wave> 2mm in the lead II, III, and aVf (p pulmonale). Left atrial enlargement produces a P wave that is broad and double-peaked in lead II (P mitrale). Usually, the P axis is between o0 and 750

The PR interval is the time between the onset of atrial depolarization and the onset of ventricular depolarization. It usually is 0.10 to 0.20 sec. Prolongation defines 1 st degree atrioventricular block.

The QRS complex represents ventricular depolarization. The Q wave is an initial downward deflection. Normal Q wave lasts

<0.05 sec in all lead except in Vi-3 I which the Q wave is considered abnormal, indicating part or current infaction. The R wave is the 1st upward deflection; criteria for average height or size are not absolute, but the taller R may cause by ventricular hypertrophy. A 2nd upward deflection in a QRS complex is design R1 . The S wave is the 2nd downward deflection. Typically, the QRS interval is 0.07 to 0.10 sec

The QT interval is the time between the onset of ventricular depolarization and the end of ventricular repolarization; the QT interval must correlate with heart rate.

The ST segment represents completed ventricular myocardial depolarization. Normally, it is horizontal along the baseline of the PR (TP) interval or slightly off the baseline.

The T wave reflects ventricular repolarization. It usually takes the same direction as the QRS complex.

The U wave appears uncommonly in parsons who have hypokalemia, hypomagnesemia, or ischemia.

Interpretation of Abnormal ECG component

1. P wave is abnormal

The possible causes are left or right hypertrophy, atrial escapes, or ectopic beat.

2. P wave absent

The possible causes are atrial fibrillation, sinus node exit block, hyperkalemia

3. P-P varying

Possibly due to a sinus arrhythmia

4. PR *interval long*

Possible reasons are first-degree atrioventricular block, Mobitz type 1 atrioventricular block or multifocal atrial tachycardia

5. QRS *complex wide*

Possible causes are right or left bundle branch block, ventricular flutter, fibrillation or hyperkalemia

6. QT *interval short*

Possible reasons are hyperkalemia, Hypermagnesemia. Grave's diseases, and digoxin drug

7. ST-*segment elevation*

Possible causes are myocardial ischemia, acute myocardial infarction, left bundle branch block, acute pericarditis, left ventricular hypertrophy, hyperkalemia, pulmonary embolism, digoxin drug, normal variation, especially in athletics heart syndrome.

8. ST-segment depression

Possible causes are myocardial ischemia. Acute posterior myocardial infarction, digoxin drug; ventricular hypertrophy; pulmonary embolism; left bundle branch block; and right bundle block

9. T wave tall

Possible causes are hyperkalemia, acute myocardiac infarction, left bundle branch block, stroke, and ventricular hypertrophy.

10. T wave small, flattened or inverted

Possible causes are myocardiac ischemia, age, race, hyperventilation, anxiety, drinking hot or cold beverages, left ventricular hypertrophy, certain drugs e.g., digoxin, pericarditis, pulmonary embolism, conduction disturbance, and electrolyte disturbances.

11. U *wave prominent*

Possible causes are hypokalemia, hypomanesemia, and ischemia.

CHAPTER 30

15 powerful tips for being productive with Apple Watch

*D*o you want to get the most of your new Apple Watch? Here are another 15 of our favorite power user tips for being prolific. The Apple Watch isn't just about exercise alone. You can use the wearable device to become more industrious, both with work and everything else you do in life. These tips will help.

1. Cover the screen to turn it off

Until Cupertino releases an Apple Watch 5 with built-in an always-on display mode that doesn't derange your battery, it's best to turn off the display quickly whenever not in use. You can also so just by covering the Watch with your palm.

2. Double-press the Digital Crown to swap between the Apple watch face and last app

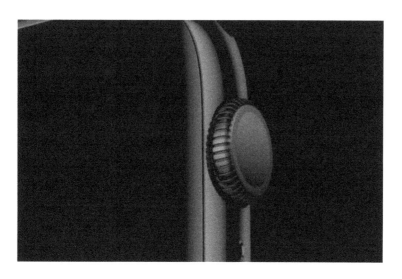

Digital Crown ring

The Digital Crown hides one of the Apple Watch's few multitasking capabilities:

double-press it on the clock face, and you'll bounce to the most-recently app used.

Double-press the Digital Crown in Watch app, and you'll return to the clock face. It's a fast way to jump around the Watch's interface without having to return to the home screen first.

3. Swipe down to dismiss notifications

Has a notification popped up on your new Watch screen that you don't want to do with right now? Just swipe down or scroll down with the Digital Crown, from the top of the screen to dismiss it.

Tip: You can force Touch in Notification Center itself to discharge all your notifications.)

4. View all websites on your Watch face

The ability to view any sites on Apple Watch is relatively new and innovative. No, the wearable Apple watch doesn't have a built-in website. However, you can see any website when you receive a link through text or mail. You can also use gestures to navigate around web pages, use Google Search, and clear website information with relative ease, all from your Apple Watch.

5. Preview your full messages in Notification Center

As long as you haven't opened the app, your notifications are from; they still live in your Apple Watch's Notification Center.

When you swipe down from the clock face and tap on a notification, you can view the entire message without it dismissing the information — or it being "seen" as read on the other end.

Practically, it means you can read messages that come in without letting the recipient know you've read it. For me, this allows quickly check for work or personal emergencies without having to signal to the other person that I've read it and am aware of the problem. Yes, I could do, in essence, the same thing by turning read receipts off entirely. Still, I like having receipts on during the workday — I don't want to be available 24/7 if it's not an emergency.

Alternatively, this is a great feature to quickly scan messages you've missed without having to duck into their respective apps. And see something without marking it as read so that you can triage it later.

6. Raise to speak to Siri

No need to have to say "Hey Siri" for the Apple watch voice assistant to get to work.

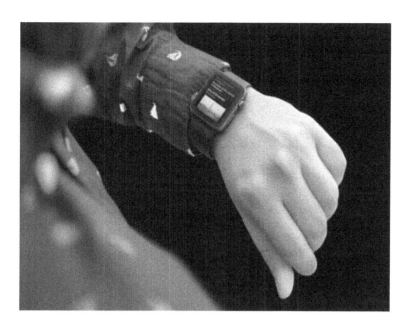

Raise to speak

As an alternative, just raise your Watch and begin to speak. This little change should make it simpler to use Siri and perhaps make it more useful.

7. When in doubt, Force Touch

You can't find a setting in the watch app. pressing firmly on display: Chances are, those features possibly will be hidden behind a Force Touch. You can also change your clock face, timer modes, create new messages or emails, send locations, or view details. Experiment and find out! There's a list of most of the force touch options for your Watch.

8. Yes, the Siri watch face is getting smarter

Initially introduced with Watch OS 4, the Siri watch face uses machine learning language to individualize the content it displays. Over time, the face suggests appropriate content and shortcuts based on what you're doing.

Siri watch face

For an instant, you might see a link to your favorite podcast pop up around the time you leave work every day. You'll likely receive a notice on the Siri watch face each time your favorite sports team is about to play. The Siri watch face works with original and third-party apps.

9. Maximize Do Not Disturb mode

The function of Do Not Disturb, as the name implied, is to keep your Watch collecting notifications without actually notifying you. That might sound strange when you're in a meeting, during sleeping or at the movies, or in a place where you don't want noise. The haptics inconveniency you, but you don't need a list of everything you might have missed in the meantime, Do Not Disturb is just what you need.

10. Selective about notification haptics

Although I like being able to see most of my notifications in the Notification Center on the Apple Watch, I don't need to get alerted for all of them. You can select which notifications buzz or beep you by going into the Apple Watch app on your iPhone. Tapping Notifications, selecting the specific setting you *wish to adjust, and then tapping Custom to customize your alert settings.*

It's worth noting that only some apps allow us to have control over whether you can enable sound or haptic alerts. However, third-party apps are limited to a simple "mirror iPhone alerts from" switch, while some built-in apps only have an "Alerts" on/off switch.

On the other hand: There's a way to turn off haptic alerts for your third-party apps without disabling warnings exclusively. On your iPhone device, open Settings and navigate to

Notifications. Choose the app you don't want to be physically alerted about, and turn off Sounds.

11. App not responding? Time for a force quit

If an app on your Apple Watch is creepy or downright frozen, there's a way how to shut it down without getting to restart your Watch.

In the errant app, hold down the side button until you see the Power off-screen, and then hold the side button again to return to your Watch's home screen.

12. Customize Control Center

Control Center in Watch OS 5 added the capability to customize the layout of the buttons.

The functionality makes it faster to get to your most important features. Still, you can modify *the button layouts to suit the needs for a specific day.*

 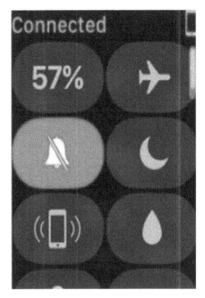

Apple Watch control center

13. Save battery life by disabling Activate on Wrist Raise

There are times when you want enabling Wrist Raise — which wakes your Apple Watch when you turn it toward you. It's imperative to note that having this on will kill the Apple Watch battery much more rapidly. Fortunately, you can turn it off.

On your Apple Watch, go to Settings > General > Activate on Wrist Raise and toggle the switch off.

14. Find your phone using your Watch

If your iPhone recurrently goes missing, you don't have to rush to your computer and iCloud.com to find out where it is. Instead, you also can use your Watch.

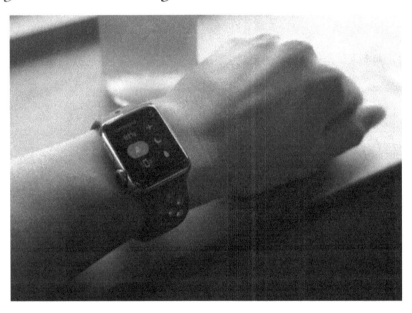

Find iPhone on Apple Watch

Unlike Find My iPhone, your Watch's search feature won't activate iCloud emails, saying your device has sent a noise. It's a much more relaxed and less complicated process.

15. Make multiple copies of the same clock face

You can customize a single clock face to your choosing — you can make various models of the same clock face, each with multiple complications. This option is especially useful if you want another watch face for exercising than everyday use.

To set-up, this, press firmly on your Apple Watch's clock face until you see the "Customize" option, and then swipe to the left until you see the plus button. Tap the button to create a new clock face you like. You can also remove clock faces you don't want to use any longer from the screen by swiping up on the front.

Conclusion

Thank you again for downloading this book!

I hope this book was able to help you to use your Apple watch effectively. Finally, if you enjoyed this book, please take the time to share your thoughts and post a review on Amazon. It'd be much appreciated!

Thank you and good luck

About the Author

Philip Knoll is CEO of techguideblog , the publishing company that published several IT books. He worked at Inte-route, Europe's largest voice and data network provider. Before Inte-route, he was working as a senior network engineer for Globtel Internet, a significant Internet and Telephony Services Provider to the market. He has been working with Linux for more than 10 years putting a strong accent on security for protecting vital data from hackers and ensuring good quality services for internet customers. Moving to VoIP services he had to focus even more on security as sensitive billing data is most often stored on servers with public IP addresses. He has been studying QoS implementations on Linux to build different types of services for IP customers and also to deliver good quality for them and for VoIP over the publicInternet.Philip has also been program ming educational software's with Perl, PHP, and Smarty for over 7 years mostly developing in-house management interfaces for IP and VoIP services.

Bonus book for buying this book.

This is the link;

https://techguideblog.net/free-ebook-60-minutes-apple-watch-guide/

Our website is http//www.techguideblog.net

You should check it out and let me know what you think. I keep a blog there for our efficient interaction. I like to invite you follow my journey, by signing up my free newsletter. If you subscribed you get free copy of my books.mp3, pdf files, and tutorials

The list of my favorite online tools, plus notification of free future kindles book and offers. Pleases, if you're interested signup

www.ingramcontent.com/pod-product-compliance
Lightning Source LLC
Chambersburg PA
CBHW031548080326
40690CB00054B/588